MASS COMMUNICATION & SOCIETY

Volume 5, Number 1, 2002 • Winter

SPECIAL ISSUE:
International Communication History

GUEST EDITORS' NOTE
Hazel Dicken-Garcia and K. Viswanath
   An Idea Whose Time Has Come: International Communication History   1

ARTICLES
Allen W. Palmer
   Negotiation and Resistance in Global Networks:
   The 1884 International Meridian Conference   7

Hanno Hardt
   Reading the Russian Revolution: International
   Communication Research and the Journalism
   of Lippmann and Merz   25

Jennifer Ostini and Anthony Y. H. Fung
   Beyond the Four Theories of the Press:
   A New Model of National Media Systems   41

Catherine A. Luther
   National Identities, Structure, and Press Images of Nations:
   The Case of Japan and the United States   57

Scott Laderman
   Shaping Memory of the Past:
   Discourse in Travel Guidebooks for Vietnam   87

Mass Communication & Society Division Information

Division Head
  Paul S. Voakes, *Indiana University*

Division Vice Head
  Kathy Brittain McKee, *Berry College*

Secretary and Newsletter Editor
  Dane Claussen, *Point Park College*

Research Committee Chairs
  Janet Bridges, *University of Louisiana-Lafayette*
  John Beatty, *LaSalle University*

Teaching Standards Committee Chairs
  Jennifer Greer, *University of Nevada at Reno*
  Stacey Cone, *University of Iowa*

Professional Freedom and Responsibility Committee Chair
  Lois A. Boynton, *University of North Carolina-Chapel Hill*

Graduate Student Liaison
  Juanita Darling, *University of North Carolina-Chapel Hill*

Webmaster
  Thomas Gould, *Kansas State University*

Archivist
  George Gladney, *University of Wyoming*

Immediate Past Head
  Daniel A. Panici, *University of Southern Maine*

Visit Mass Communication & Society's website at http://aejmc-mcs.org

GUEST EDITORS' NOTE

An Idea Whose Time Has Come: International Communication History

Hazel Dicken-Garcia
School of Journalism and Mass Communication
University of Minnesota

K. Viswanath
National Cancer Institute

With great appreciation to the authors represented here and to reviewers who have assisted us, we present this collection of articles devoted to international communication history. Although researchers have long produced work related to international communication history, this special issue of *Mass Communication & Society* marks the first treatment of the subject as a distinct body of knowledge and area of inquiry. The subject matter of these five articles spans approximately a century, with the first focusing on the 1884 conference on international time reckoning and the last focusing on a collective memory, still under "construction," of the 1960s and 1970s war in Vietnam. The articles reflect shifting paradigms in multiple realms—international affairs, theoretical frameworks, types of questions posed, for example—and thus, by their nature, point up the richness of areas awaiting study. International communication history transcends conceptions of intercultural communication, which, of course, is related, and it transcends conceptions of histories of individual nations' press systems, which, of course, are crucial parts of its foundation. Although the study of international communication history seems to us an idea whose time is long

---

Requests for reprints should be sent to Hazel Dicken-Garcia, School of Journalism and Mass Communication, University of Minnesota, 111 Murphy Hall, 206 Church Street, S.E., Minneapolis, MN 55455. E-mail: dicke0003@umn.edu

overdue, we regard the beginning of the 21st century as particularly auspicious for calling attention to this frontier for scholarly exploration.

Globalization highlights the need to study communication processes across time as well as across space. At the most basic level is a need to examine the historical role of media, media organizations, and communication in relation to global issues of concern today. Kumar (1995) laid an important foundation for exploring international communication history with work that raises questions relating to turning points in modern societies' histories: What has been the transformation of work and organization in the global community? What have been crises of political ideologies and cultural beliefs? How has communication figured in all these areas and especially what have been patterns concerning information and communication revolutions? Kumar (1995), in fact, suggested the centrality of communication to all phenomena marking postindustrial theory (pp. 6–35).

In a similar vein, Stamps's (1995) question about how economics, media, and politics intertwine to create personal and social consequences calls attention to the ubiquitous role of communication (pp. ix, 23). For, as Kumar noted (citing Bell, 1973), current society is defined by present methods of acquiring, processing, and distributing information, and new information technology is potentially applicable to every sector of society. This "revolutionary transformation of modern society" (3) requires study of that process of transformation historically and the role of communication in forging and shaping it. Revolutionary transformations, such as Kumar referred to, have changed media and media organizations—and, in turn, altered institutional arrangements within which media interact. What are those histories?

Historically, communication in the global community reflects shifting balances of power among nations and thus changing paradigms in international affairs. Such shifts, of course, alter milieus in which communication and political activities occur; consequently, patterns of behavior and communication in international affairs are always being reshaped. What has been the history of such patterns and how have shifts in political power shaped international communication across time, and vice versa? Furthermore, how have such shifts affected the study and historical knowledge of international communication? As nations verge on revolutionary change or throes of paradigm-shattering developments, what accounts of histories are generated and used—how and for what purposes? How do the accounts become reconfigured as events unfold? Analysis of communication, historically, across these accounts can reveal insights that may inform future global policies.

A dominant theme permeating all the articles in this issue is the role of communication in shaping international affairs; a secondary theme—obvious in all except the first—is the Cold War paradigm in international affairs, and related to this is a submerged theme throughout of an East–West dichotomy. But these few articles only begin to scratch the surface of a vast area awaiting exploration. Study of turning points represented by paradigm shifts, and what preceded and succeeded them, can provide a basis for building understanding of communication in the global community in the present and future. Equally compelling as the history of patterns of communication in shifting political paradigms of international affairs, the very questions posed about international communication over time can reveal changes (or reconstructions) in historical knowledge—and why reconstructions occur. Meanings of important terms in the international arena change, as do national consciousnesses and national identities. Indeed, changes in questions about international communication over time provide clues to changing national identities. In addition to these, the following list indicates only a few broad areas of needed research:

1. Comparative historical research to test applicability of models across differing political and social systems; "universals," or commonalities, across nations and time, in communication and its history; convergences and divergences across national boundaries and what may be learned from these.

2. History of the role of communication intersecting nations and cultures, contexts surrounding the structuring and reconstructing of policies; and analyses of communication in times of crises.

3. History of the relationship of communication to national (and international) identities, particularly how people of any nation "identify" their own and other nations. How have differing cultures constructed their own histories and "traits" of other cultures? What is the history of patterns of communication development in different countries, and what might be learned from analyses of similarities and differences?

4. Shifts in values globally. In 1971, Inglehart predicted values in advanced industrial nations would shift from materialism and economic and physical security to freedom, quality of life, and self-expression—implying trends from an authoritarian toward a democratization model, higher levels of education, and changed nature of work—requiring more specialized knowledge (Abramson & Inglehart, 1995/1998, p. 1). To what extent has this occurred?

What are transforming mechanisms that conduct values and ideologies, and through what processes? And how do larger constructs, such as "democracy," relate to those, in what forms—and how do those vary over time? How have such constructs as race, gender, class, ethnicity, and tribalism been used and understood through time and across cultures? That is, how are such constructs understood across national boundaries? How do changes in meaning and usage of such issues affect international relations?

This collection of articles does not, of course, address all such questions, but it represents a beginning of a long-overdue scholarly inquiry. The collection, as noted, spans roughly a century and, as implied earlier, it also roughly represents shifting paradigms in international communication interests, theories, and global alignments. The first article points up the far-reaching consequences of "mechanical time reckoning" at an international 1884 conference marking a culmination of developments linking nations across the 19th century with special implications for communication. The first steamship to cross the Atlantic in the 1830s, for example, led to establishment of the first news bureaus and correspondents in foreign capitals; editor James Gordon Bennett went to Europe on the steamer's return trip to establish those bureaus and correspondents. Dell'Orto (in press) wrote about how those first correspondents "constructed" for American readers the nations on which they reported. The implications of that history reach even to today, for how the unknown was then made familiar and given meaning set a basis for continuing international affairs.

Soon after the steamship speeded transportation across oceans, the telegraph linked the world community—commodifying time, author Allen Palmer (this issue) writes, as an unexpected consequence—and this was followed in the 1860s by the trans-Atlantic cable. Among its far-reaching implications, Palmer writes, "[T]he 1884 International Meridian Conference in Washington, DC [on world time zones], formalized the new *standard temporal reference framework* [which was] needed for the kind of mutual interdependence that would make social and economic intercourse possible across international frontiers" (p. 10). "What is today narrowly defined as 'mass communication' is an outgrowth of the new social formations arising from the convergence of new technologies and the audiences they defined as markets" (p. 9). A time system agreed on by nations symbolizes interdependence of nations, interdependence of media and politics across international boundaries, and a foundation from which international communication research sprang.

These phenomena figure to a greater or lesser degree in the article by Hanno Hardt (this issue) about a 1920 study of *New York Times* coverage of the Russian Revolution. This article connects to Palmer's argument as Hardt notes that "the history of foreign affairs coverage as a reflection of U.S. foreign policy offers an example of the growing interdependence of media and politics in the 20th century" (p. 27). With urbanization, industrialization, spread of large-circulation newspapers, and "America's extended involvement in world affairs," Hardt writes, the media increasingly played "a major role in producing the images of people and events that would determine individual and collective judgments" while serving "specific cultural or political purposes" (p. 27). He notes, "The field of international and comparative communication studies matured alongside these mounting public demands ... for information and explanation, which helped reinforce the international dimension of American mass communication research" (p. 27). The article shows work that clearly foreshadows the Cold War and emphasizes the role of communication in shaping international affairs.

The article by Jennifer Ostini and Anthony Fung about the four theories of the press exemplifies shifting paradigms—in international affairs, theoretical frameworks, and lines of inquiry. With a critique of Cold-War–shaped theories—theories "constrained by the ideology and historical circumstances of its inception," including a set of Western assumptions (p. 45)—the authors propose a new model and offer an illustrative case study. Significantly, they insist that "[i]ncorporation of value systems of individual journalists" who report international affairs "allows for differentiation between countries" while avoiding treatment of them "as similar on the basis of state or economic system" (p. 55).

Fung and Ostini introduce the importance of value systems shaping journalists' reporting as a significant influence in international affairs—and international communication history. The ensuing article also alludes to value systems in an emphasis on national identities, which, Catherine Luther argues, have shaped international communication and relations over time. Addressing whether national identities change over time and, if so, to what such change is related, Luther found consistent national images (national identities) in media content, but some shifts reflected international relationships.

Reflecting shifting theoretical paradigms across the century, Luther's article raises fundamental questions about national identities, communication, and shifting international power arrangements, whereas the final article, by Scott Laderman, suggests how national identities may be constructed and reified through media treatment of specific historical international events. Arguing that media content fundamentally shapes collective memories of events, Laderman focuses on how tour guidebook accounts help shape collective memory about an event (Vietnam War) that continues to mark an epoch in international history.

Of special interest to us, these articles taken together show that recent major issues in international communication and international relations occupying scholars' and practitioners' attention have much earlier origins. For example, Palmer's article, which outlines the struggle among various colonial powers to determine the location of the International Meridian, mirrors in some ways contemporary struggles over global treaties, such as the North American Free Trade Agreement and the World Trade Organization. Interestingly, one motivation of the original treaty to determine the international meridian is commerce, and at least one consequence—intended or otherwise—is integration of global markets. It is also instructive to note that the origins of a major international treaty lie in a struggle for control among elite powers, and this continues to be the case today. Clearly, treaties have consequences beyond their own times, and we have only now begun to understand the impacts of many.

Similarly, the coverage of international news in local media systems, a topic of great interest and controversy in the 1970s and 1980s, was a concern at least 7 decades earlier, as Hardt's article demonstrates. That article, based on an early study by Lippmann and Merz (1920), suggests that the roots of the modern history of international communication research lie in the effort at self-criticism in American journalism. The premise raises the question of what happened to this culture of self-criticism. Recent history surrounding the debate of the New World Information and Communication Order suggests that American media were less than hospitable to the criticism of their coverage from academia and activists. Why did this tradition cited by Hardt not continue?

These articles represent not only different methods and types of analysis; they also exemplify multilevel and situational approaches that enrich our understanding of media in international relations. For example, authors Ostini and Fung call for the inclusion of professional values of individual reporters to be incorporated into the model explaining state–press relations—thereby recommending a multilevel approach. Luther's article argues for a more dynamic analysis of study of media images by examining the conditions under which shifts in media construction of national images may or may not occur.

But the largest question these articles raise may be: Have we learned anything from history? More important, do we know enough about international communication history to draw any lessons from it? This special issue, we hope, is the beginning of mining the history of international communication.

REFERENCES

Abramson, P. R., & Inglehart, R. (1998). *Value change in global perspective.* Ann Arbor: The University of Michigan Press. (Original work published 1995)

Bell, D. (1973). *The coming of post-industrial society.* New York: Basic Books.

Dell'Orto, G. (in press). *Giving meanings to the world: The first U.S. foreign correspondents, 1838–1859.* Westport, CT: Greenwood.

Kumar, K. (1995). *From post-industrial to post-modern society: New theories of the contemporary world.* Cambridge, MA: Blackwell.

Lippmann, W., & Merz, C. (1920). A test of the news. *The New Republic, 23*(296), 1–42.

Stamps, J. (1995). *Unthinking modernity: Innis, McLuhan, and the Frankfurt School.* Montreal, Canada: McGill-Queen's University Press.

Negotiation and Resistance in Global Networks: The 1884 International Meridian Conference

Allen W. Palmer
Communications Department
Brigham Young University

One of the first dialogues about international standards of communication was at an 1884 conference in Washington, DC, convened to discuss reforming time standards and designate an international meridian. The emergence of both telegraph and railroad systems had been important precursors of national time zone systems in North America and Europe, but creation of an international time system required unprecedented cooperation over divergent national interests through expanding networks of scientists. The international time system arose from the pervasive influence of the shipping industry and its innovations in science, especially astronomical innovations in reckoning longitude by chronometers. International time reform faced obstacles from competing national, economic, and cultural interests. The selection of Greenwich Observatory near London as the international meridian showed tacit acceptance among negotiators of a shift to a scientific center of global interests, in spite of resistance from France, which hoped to establish Paris as the international meridian, as well as the metric system as the basis of international exchange.

Technological innovations in shipping and the changing role of international science in the mid-19th century brought far-reaching changes in relations among nations. The melding of relations among previously isolated nations into a coherent global network resulted from intermingling both their shared interests and intractable differences through technology. Beginning with the railroad and telegraph, towns and cities were brought closer together as a nation, regardless of whether participants were reluctant or enthusiastic. Railroad

---

Requests for reprints should be sent to Allen W. Palmer, Department of Communication, Brigham Young University, E-509 Harris Fine Arts Center, Provo, UT 84602-6403. E-mail: allen_palmer@byu.edu

and telegraph companies, as powerful corporate utilities, achieved a kind of quasi-government authority in the era's *zeitgeist*—unbridled optimism in empire building.

The railroad and telegraph systems were important in empire building because only these kinds of agencies could successfully bring technological innovation to previously isolated communities. Government officers were not equal to the task, even though subsequent political developments gave the initiative for building a national network infrastructure back to government (e.g., the interstate highway system in the 1950s and the electronic Internet in the 1980s and 1990s). Although railroad and telegraph systems formed the mechanical backbone of the national communication network, they do not entirely explain the expansion of international communication networks because railroad systems did not cross international frontiers in the mid-19th century, except in a few contiguous border areas, such as between the United States and Canada. Even in locations where geography did not prohibit it, the assimilation of railway systems into cooperative international ventures was slowed by incompatible rail gauges and business interests (Taylor & Neu, 1956).

The two main arguments of this article deal with how technological innovations opened new international networks through the shipping industry and international science, and how such innovations were assimilated in the often-fitful contingencies of negotiation—and resistance—among reluctant participants. The choice of Greenwich Observatory near London as the international meridian in October 1884 is evidence of the importance of both shipping and science in establishing early international relations. This decision not only signaled global predominance of the British naval fleet on the oceans, but it was the demarcation of a *scientific* center of global influence against competing historical, religious, and national claims to cultural authority. What came in the bargain, however, was affirmation that "the clock, not the steamengine, is the key machine of the modern industrial age" (Mumford, 1963, p. 14).

Dramatic changes in the temporality of mechanical timekeeping happened at the same time as key innovations in mass communication, both developments in the urban transformation of Western Europe and North America in the 19th century. It was precisely the changing density and quickening pace of urban life that required progressively higher levels of public coordination of mechanical time and mass communication (Lowe, 1982).

The practical decisions about how to proceed toward time reform and where to place the international meridian were remarkable because so few people had an explicit vision of international time, and no political mechanisms then existed to enact such reform. Much as the railroad and telegraph barons exerted their will to conquer the American frontier, the decision to make Greenwich the common meridian was tantamount to deciding where time would begin on the international frontier.

TIME AS ARTIFACT IN COMMUNICATION HISTORY

In the same way that the clock is selectively defined as an instrument of social control, time is not frequently considered in the historical formation of international networks of communication (Bartky, 1984, 1985, 1989; Butler, 1990; Carey, 1989; Creet, 1990; Innis, 1991; Landes, 1983; Smith, 1976; Stephens, 1989). Both communication media and the clock "frame and facilitate" social perceptions (Lowe, 1982, p. 1). Changing standards of time measurement implied the reconstruction of authority people used to control the routines of their lives and their work (Battagalia, 1992; Beniger, 1986; Innis, 1991; Thompson, 1967). Mechanical apparatuses for timekeeping meant "supplanting nature and God with clocks and watches . . . [and] with secular authorities based on efficiency and convenience" (O'Malley, 1990, p. ix). Yet, even an otherwise artificial framework for time became an important reference point because:

> Only within . . . temporal structure does everyday life retain . . . its accent of reality. Thus in cases where I may be "disoriented" . . . I feel an almost instinctive urge to "reorient" myself within the temporal structure of everyday life. I look at my watch and try to recall what day it is. By those acts alone I re-enter the reality of everyday life. (Berger & Luckmann, 1967, p. 28)

Mechanical time reckoning also had far-reaching economic consequences. Railways and telegraph "were the first to feel the need to find new modes of organization adapted to the management of the continuous circulation of goods, services, and information on a large scale" (Mattelart, 2000, p. 10). In this broader view, international time standards were naturalized as part of the market mentality that both rationalized the merchant as a citizen of the world, and "the deployment of technological networks [that] perpetuated . . . worldwide economic integration" (Mattelart, 2000, p. 6). What is today narrowly defined as mass communication is an outgrowth of the new social formations arising from the convergence of new technologies and the audiences they defined as markets.

Clearly, international time standards challenged the comprehension of the lay person. Although ship navigators knew they would gain a full calendar day on sailing a course westward on the seas, thanks to Magellan in 1522, time reckoning still defied public credulity. Jules Verne captured the general confusion in his serialized novel *Around the World in 80 Days,* published in the Paris magazine *Temps* (1872). The account of Phineas Fogg's surprise victory in the global race because of confusion over the calendar appeared a full decade before the official placement of the International Date Line in the mid–Pacific Ocean by the delegates at the International Meridian Conference. Until Greenwich was designated as the international meridian, a boundary between "east" and "west" at the 180th parallel would not have been possible.

In effect, the 1884 International Meridian Conference in Washington, DC, formalized the new standard temporal reference framework (Zerubavel, 1982). Such a framework was needed for the kind of mutual interdependence that would make social and economic intercourse possible across international frontiers.

Emerging Need for Time Standards

By the 1870s, international commerce had been responsible for expanding relations between nations. International agreements were being drafted to regulate postal and telegraph traffic. The International Telegraph Union was formed in 1865 and the Universal Postal Union was established in 1875, both making communication across distances easier for the middle classes.

Frequent travelers and railway managers confronted practical problems of time reckoning. Because different American railroads used different calculations of "solar time," most central rail terminals prominently displayed numerous different clocks reporting different times based on the separate rail operations connecting at the station.

Although the railway and telegraph were ultimately responsible for the need to standardize the national time system, individual railroad managers were generally disinterested in initiating national time reform on their own. Some felt it was a problem better handled by government. Others saw no practical benefit of time reform outside of the railway system itself (American Society of Civil Engineers, 1889). A more immediate concern of railroad entrepreneurs was the problem of railway safety. Reports of several spectacular crashes between trains sharing the same rail lines forced local railway officials to confront the problem of coordination as a means of control of new unwieldy mechanical systems (Beniger, 1986).

Charles F. Dowd (1870), the principal of Temple Grove Ladies Seminary in Saratoga Springs, New York, began a vigorous campaign on his own to reform the railway time system in the United States. He was baffled by the patchwork of four different time systems he encountered in his travel from Portland, Maine, to Buffalo, New York. He was likewise bemused that a telegraph message could be sent from east to west and arrive earlier than its original time of transmission.

The epitome of Victorian virtue, Dowd was a person who "liked order, he disliked confusion," wrote his son (C. N. Dowd, 1930, p. 5). "It is not strange that the confusion of [the railroad system's] multiple time standards should seem to him absurd" (p. 5). His proposal for a railroad time system employed dual times—a local time based on the position of the sun, and an average time based on a nearby city. Such a dual-time system required adapting watches and clocks with an extra set of hands to distinguish the difference between the two fixed times. Although railroad managers debated the system for 13 years, it was never officially adopted because it was considered to be cumbersome and difficult to manage.

Dual-hand watches and clocks are today considered valuable artifacts of the failed time system.

Astronomy and Time Reckoning at Sea

The problems of time reckoning on land and at sea were generally approached as two separate issues. Three advocates who believed it was possible to solve them together were Cleveland Abbe of the U.S. Signal Office and an officer in the American Meteorological Association; William F. Allen, a former resident engineer of the Camden and Amboy railway system and editor of the U.S. railway time tables; and Sandford Fleming, chief engineer of the Intercolonial Railway in Canada, who had recently completed surveys for new railway lines in remote western Canada. All three were advocates of national time standards and saw reasons to extend the reform internationally. Fleming, in particular, was tireless in his pursuit of international time reform (Creet, 1990). He was committed to raising public consciousness about time management problems and spoke frequently to scientific groups, government agents, and the public at large.

Scientists in Europe had long anticipated the need for coordination of the measurement of time, but were generally ambivalent about their responsibility to take action that might bring about such reform. As early as 1800, La Place cited the need for a common meridian:

> It is desirable that all of the nations of Europe, in place of arranging geographical longitude from their own observatories, should agree to compute it from the same meridian, one indicated by nature herself. . . . Such an arrangement would introduce into the science of geography the same uniformity which is already enjoyed in the calendar and the arithmetic, and, extended to the numerous objects of their mutual relations, would make of the diverse peoples one family only. (Wheeler, 1885, p. 30)

Through the work of astronomers in both Paris and Greenwich, the geographical precision of cartography had steadily improved, but different nations preferred designating their own meridian. Among the meridians suggested in various scientific venues were the Paris Observatory, the Great Pyramid of Giza in Egypt, the Jerusalem temple, the city of Rome, and several islands and ocean locations considered more deliberately "neutral."

Scientifically, it mattered little, if at all, which meridian was used for the measurement. International coordination depended only on a common point of reference. Accurate longitudes were easily fixed by comparing local time based on the position of the sun at high noon (corrected for the Earth's wobble) with the simultaneous time calculation at an astronomical observatory. One hour difference in the two readings equals 15 degrees longitude. The main problem for early astronomers and navigators was to make a reliable timepiece that would keep accurate reckoning in spite of the erratic movement and general abuse on shipboard. If the British had an advantage as clockmakers, it was because of the advancement of metalwork crafts developed early in the Industrial Era (E. P. Thompson, 1967). Before the mid-19th century, watches were partly ornamental and partly utilitarian, but they were gradually to become essential for those associated with transportation, or who depended on it for commerce.

The British Parliament offered a reward in 1714 for the first clockmaker to "discover the longitude at sea" (Howse, 1980, p. 50). Dozens of chronometers were shipped in wooden crates to and from the West Indies to compare their precision. After devoting 50 years to improving his chronometers, clockmaker John Harrison won the reward in 1765. However, measurement of longitude through astronomical observations alone became feasible by the 1760s with the invention of the sextant and the publication of celestial tables in Greenwich Observatory's annual *Nautical Almanac.*

Greenwich Observatory provided a time signal in 1833 to the British navy with the manual use of a moving "time ball" visible by ship navigators anchored in the nearby Thames River. The ball was eventually wired for electrical control in 1855, and the observatory then began using telegraph signals to control the movement of the balls on various remote sites, including the roof of the London telegraph headquarters and at coastal lighthouses. Eventually, even the German Empire was added to the British telegraph time-ball system, also using Greenwich as the reference point. London clockmakers also used Greenwich time signals for timekeeping for mail deliveries using horse-drawn stage service. Clockmakers were asked eventually to subsidize the observatory for the service (Meadows, 1975).

One person who resisted international time reform was Sir George Airy, British astronomer royal at the Greenwich Observatory and one of the scientists known for advances in calculating longitude using chronometers (clocks) for the British naval fleet. During Airy's long tenure as manager of the Greenwich Observatory, he witnessed the remarkable development of time signals using everything from rockets, time balls, and electric signals distributed to telegraph offices, post offices, and lighthouses (Howse, 1997).

Airy was a staunch defender of using the Greenwich Observatory as the standard of longitudinal measurement for the British system. He noted in correspondence to his supervisors in the British admiralty: "The meridional [sic] system is sacredly preserved" (Meadows, 1975, p. 4). Renowned in British science for adapting the chronometer for longitude measurements over land, he directed his staff's experiments to determine the longitude difference between Greenwich and other nearby locations. Eventually they measured the distance to observatories in Paris and in Russia.

A Pulkovo, Russia, astronomical facility was established as the meridian for standard time throughout Russia. To coordinate timekeeping between Britain and Russia, astronomers at Greenwich shipped 42 chronometers across the North Sea 16 times to make precise measurements.

Time signals from Greenwich Observatory were also valued by British clockmakers for calibration and repair of privately owned timepieces. Airy despaired of routine clerical work required to satisfy local timekeepers, and he was suspicious local clockmakers were bribing his observatory staff members to perform unauthorized work on timepieces (Meadows, 1975).

Indeed, Airy aspired to engage his observatory staff in more challenging science. He recognized the significant gap in the preponderance of mundane, almost clerical functions performed by his British observatory compared to what he regarded as more advanced scientific work at the Paris observatory. Airy complained in an annual government report that the expectations imposed on his staff prevented expansion into astrophysics: "The observatory was considered rather as a place for managing government chronometers than as a place of science" (Airy, 1896, p. 124). Concerning the need to move toward more scientific approaches of astronomy, he wrote:

> Still the question has not infrequently presented itself to me, whether the duties to which I allude have not, by force of circumstances, become too exclusive; whether the cause of science might not gain if, as in the Imperial Observatory in Paris for instance, the higher branches of mathematical physics should take their place by the side of Observatory routine. (Meadows, 1975, p. 5)

As much as he wanted to expand the scientific work of the observatory, he was adamant in the practical value of Greenwich for British timekeeping, but curiously, he was unwilling to promote public time reform beyond Britannia's own borders.

Internationalizing the Telegraph System

On the Western shores of the Atlantic, when Samuel F. B. Morse proposed building a telegraph line from Washington to Baltimore, he asked Congress for financial support in 1842. His proposal was denounced by critics as a waste of public funds. However, international expansion of the telegraph soon became a question of business speculation because of the appetite in the American business centers for news from Europe.

Even though the first underwater telegraph line ran under the North Sea and connected astronomical observatories in Greenwich and Paris in 1851, the transAtlantic cable linking America with Europe was perhaps the single most important achievement in internationalizing the time system.

There is no clear evidence that American developers of the trans-Atlantic cable were preoccupied with the potential use of the telegraph for time and longitude measurements. The Greenwich Observatory used the telegraph signal from the trans-Atlantic cable ship the *Great Eastern* to plot the ship's position in the Atlantic even before the trans-Atlantic line was complete in 1866 (Meadows, 1975). Developers, however, were primarily motivated by their hopes of cutting the time for news to travel by steamer from Europe to America by as much as 48 hr (R. L. Thompson, 1972).

One of the earliest proposals for a trans-Atlantic cable line was mentioned in the *National Telegraph Review* in July 1853, but business promoters failed to attract sufficient backing. Cyrus Field and Frederick N. Gisborne considered the proposal again in 1854 and sought the backing of telegraph inventor Morse (R. L. Thompson, 1972). Morse unwittingly hindered the trans-Atlantic cable project because of his lack of business acumen. Consummating the project involved a series of difficult business deals, including consolidation of then-independent U.S. telegraph systems into what would eventually become the American Telegraph Company. Morse was anxious to see the expansion of the telegraph technology and promised the use of his patents without charge on a line from the British Provinces in Canada to New York, and to transmit telegraph messages at half price.

Before a trans-Atlantic project materialized, another entrepreneur, businessman Perry McDonough Collins, began promoting another ambitious international telegraph scheme to tie the world together by telegraph. Collins wanted to lay a telegraph line to connect Western Union's transcontinental American line with his new line to run over land through British Columbia, Russian America (Alaska), under the Bering Strait, and overland again through Siberia to connect to a Russian line in eastern Asia. Collins's extended plan also envisioned construction of telegraph lines to Central and Latin America. Collins had obtained approval from both the American and Russian governments to begin work on the line, and he had dispatched George Kennan to begin the work in Alaska and Russia. The project was aborted in July 1866 when news spread of the successful laying of a trans-Atlantic cable (Travis, 1990).

A call for building an American observatory was published as early as 1812 to be "an appendage, if not an attribute of sovereignty" (O'Malley, 1990, p. 56). An American observatory would lessen reliance of Americans on European astronomy. As a practical matter, however, there were only a few people who questioned dependence on European, and British, time. Simon Newcomb, superintendent of the American-published *Nautical Almanac,* wrote: "Americans don't care for other nations; we can't help them, they can't help us." He observed "no more need for considering Europe in the matter [time reform] than for considering the inhabitants of Mars" (Howse, 1980, p. 134).

The commodification of time became an unexpected consequence of the international expansion of the telegraph. Samuel Langley, who later would be appointed secretary of the Smithsonian Institution, was one of the first American astronomers to distribute time in the American marketplace. Seeking financial support for the observatory, he sold telegraphic time signals from the Allegheny Observatory to a local railway line and a jewelry shop in Pittsburgh (O'Malley, 1990).

Time Reckoning in American Railroad Systems

Confusion arising from railway calculation of time in different cities was a matter of curiosity and concern for travelers and railroad operators. Coordinating time across distances was a practical problem precipitated by the amalgam of railroad and telegraph operators:

> Away from the world of telegraphs and railroad trains, there was just no reason to care. Only the railroads, the ultimate symbol of commercial expansion, progress, and the conquest of space, had the motive and the power to reform public timekeeping. (O'Malley, 1990, p. 100)

American political and government leaders kept a respectful distance from legislation dealing with time because proposals to change time standards were generally unpopular. Several preliminary initiatives to standardize time presented to Congress died from inaction or neglect. Standard time was popularly known as "railroad time" or "Vanderbilt's time" (Carey, 1989). Populist protest against standard time were part of the widespread disapproval of the blind influence wielded by the banks, the telegraph, and the railroads.

It became apparent that coordination of passenger schedules was in the railway operators' collective interest for economic reasons. Railway service was originally regarded useful for transportation of freight and mail. Transport of passengers developed rather abruptly into a source of revenue for the railway systems, but fragmentation of railway service posed a difficult obstacle for long-distance service. A contingent of railroad superintendents met in St. Louis in early 1872 to arrange the forthcoming summer rail passenger schedules between different adjoining rail lines. They formed a permanent organization called the Time-Table Convention to address the persistent discrepancies of time calculation across the United States. The name was subsequently changed to the General Time Convention, the American Railway Association, and, finally, the Association of American Railroads.

William F. Allen, the former resident engineer of the Camden and Amboy Railroad and secretary of the General Time Convention, was given the charge to develop a workable railway time proposal (J. S. Allen, 1951; W. F. Allen, 1910). His collaborative plan, discussed at length with Abbe and Fleming, among others, was accepted by the General Time Convention on October 11, 1883. It included five time "belts" in Standard Railway Time based on the 60th, 75th, 90th, 105th, and 120th meridians west of Greenwich, based approximately on longitudes of Eastern, Atlantic, Valley, Mountain, and Pacific. These divisions were to be followed later by adoption of a single standard for the continent at 70 degrees, or 6 hr, west of Greenwich. For the system to work, state and national legislatures were to be petitioned to make railway and telegraph time legal for all public and private business.

British astronomer royal Airy was among those who reacted negatively to the American railway proposal for an international time system. He advised the British government to abstain from interfering directly in public uses of time, "until the spontaneous rise of such novelties [had] become so extensive as to make it desirable that regulations should be sanctioned by superior authority" (Creet, 1990, p. 75).

Even without the imprimatur of the British astronomer royal, the railway plan was approved by the U.S. General Time Convention and implemented in the states on November 18, 1883. Of the 100 principal cities in the United States, 70 adopted Standard Railway Time immediately, and by October 1884, it had been adopted by 85% of all American towns with populations more than 10,000 (Bartky & Harrison, 1979).

Conflicts between railway companies over boundaries between systems led to the call for direct government involvement, but it required 35 years for Congress to take action. The Standard Time Act, passed on March 19, 1918, essentially sanctioned the system already in use by the railroads. The act gave the Interstate Commerce Commission the power to enforce time zone boundaries (Holbrook, 1947). Administrative decisions about changes in boundaries of American time zones are managed today by the U.S. Department of Transportation.

International Cooperation Among Scientists

With few exceptions, national government leaders were ambivalent about international scientific endeavors. Government cooperation on science hinged on the preconditions that such projects "did not cost too much, that the scientists themselves were prepared to do the work, and that nothing in the commitment trenched upon national security or sovereignty" (Lyons, 1963, pp. 228–229).

France was positioned to play a central role in negotiation of the new international standards of exchange, but had a history of marshaling communication systems into its closely held military objectives. The nation's visual semaphore signal system employing a network of towers was held closely in national service and the semaphore code itself was considered a state secret until about 1850.

France's representatives promoted worldwide adoption of the metric system as early as 1792, calling the meter a "new bond of general fraternity for the peoples who adopt it" and the "beneficial truth that will become a new link between nations and one of the most useful conquests of equality" (Mattelart, 2000, p. 5). A key obstacle in the success of the metric system was the indifference or intransigence of countries that resisted its adoption. The American Meteorological Society had accepted a challenge to promote the metric system, especially in the English-speaking countries that had resisted it.

Prior to the mid-19th century, only a few intergovernmental collaborative ventures in science existed. One of the earliest projects was an initiative to measure the size of the earth sponsored by the Prussian Institute of Geodesy in 1862, an organization that in 1867 changed its name to the International Geodetic Association.

The first global code of science occurred in 1860 when a congress of chemists convened in Karlsruhe, Germany, to clarify the general usage of a standard list of chemical symbols. Within a few years, similar congresses were convened to consider botany and horticulture (1864), geodesy (1864), astronomy (1865), pharmacy (1865), meteorology (1873), and geology (1878).

In 1889, there were 91 ancillary international meetings held in conjunction with the Paris Universal Exhibition. By the late 1880s, the Paris-based Association for Scientific Advancement (*Alliance Scientifique Universelle*) issued an identity card or passport called the "Diplome-Circulaire," which scientists carried on their foreign travels (Crawford, 1992). From such assemblies, there were 37 international cooperative agreements drafted between 1850 and 1880. Such agreements were issued by organizations like the International Telegraph Union, the General Postal Union in 1974, and the Agreement for International Regulation of Sea Routes in 1879 (Mattelart, 2000).

The problems of time reckoning were addressed at numerous international science meetings, including the International Geographical Congress in Antwerp, the International Congress for the Codification of the Law of Nations in Cologne, the International Institution for Preserving and Perfecting Weights and Measures, and national geographical societies in Madrid, Paris, Geneva, and Berlin.

The International Commission for Weights and Measures (*Bureau International des Poids et Mesures*) was located at Sevrés, just outside Paris in 1875. The congress issued the Metric Convention, a pact whose signatories agreed to adopt the metric system in return for acquiring seats on the Paris-based commission. The 2nd International Geographical Congress in Rome in 1875 first raised the possibility of international reciprocation: The French would accept Greenwich as the prime meridian if the English would adopt the metric system.

In Venice at the 3rd International Geographical Congress in 1881, there was consideration of neutral sites for the common international meridian. Scotland's royal astronomer suggested the Great Pyramid in Egypt because of its central role in Western antiquity. An Italian astronomer proposed setting the meridian in Jerusalem because of its religious significance. A Swiss representative proposed the Bering Strait as a possible meridian, based on its geographical neutrality.

Whether the scientists attending such meetings had government authority to bind their respective governments to decisions about an international time system was unclear. The Venice convention issued a call through the Italian government for a general meeting the following year to consider international time standards: "This commission should be composed of scientific members, such as geodesists and geographers, and of persons representing the interests of commerce, learning, etc." (Wheeler, 1885, p. 23). The resolution directly acknowledged: "The . . . establishment of a common initial meridian and uniform time reckoning, more than any other action of the [scientific] congress, interests the United States" (Wheeler, 1885, p. 23).

In addition to the question of setting an international meridian, other proposals were advanced in Venice pertaining to reordering time. Among those proposals was a plan for a 24-hr clock, designated time zones by dividing the earth by longitude areas, and designation of a public-time signal facility in each city and town to be connected to an observatory where time would originate.

Otto Struve, a Russian astronomer who had lobbied for adoption of a Greenwich meridian as early as 1870, had encountered early French opposition to the Greenwich proposal. Later, Struve corresponded with both Sandford Fleming and Cleveland Abbe, his former students, asking them to take up the cause of time reform. Ostensibly, it was Struve's previous encounter with the French objections to Greenwich that inspired Fleming to propose the Bering Strait as an alternative at the 1884 Washington time conference, an idea of Fleming's that had been earlier rejected by the British Association for the Advancement in Science.

An October 1883 resolution adopted by the 7th General Conference of the International Geodetic Association in Rome urged action on the problem of timekeeping regardless of the obstacles in negotiation. Standardization of exchange would require concessions: "The unification of longitude and time is desirable in the interest of science, navigation, commerce, and international communications; and the scientific and practical utility far surpasses the sacrifices necessary to attain it" (Wheeler, 1885, p. 34).

The consensus of opinion seemed to be that Greenwich was the preferred site for the designated international meridian merely as a practical matter. There were at least a dozen other meridians in use by various coalitions of nations, generally following colonial lines of naval authority. The large number of meridians was an embarrassment to astronomers, who believed a single international meridian was altogether preferable and necessary.

1884 INTERNATIONAL MERIDIAN CONFERENCE CONVENES

American scientists sought to enlist the support of the U.S. Congress to host an international time congress. Abbe petitioned Congress to sponsor a conference and Congress passed a resolution on August 3, 1882, asking the president to invite delegates from all the nations with diplomatic relations with the United States to meet in Washington to confer on the problem. The conference would be the first international meeting to be convened expressly to discuss time reform, and for which there exists an extended published account.

Meeting at the old Executive Office Building were 41 delegates from 25 nations. Ostensibly, all of the representatives dispatched to the meeting were authorized to represent their governments, but it was apparent the conference delegates were an uneven match of authority and expertise. Among them were statesmen and diplomats, astronomers and railway engineers, and naval officers. Dispatched from France were a government diplomat and the director of the Paris Observatory. There were five representatives from the United States: William F. Allen, Cleveland Abbe, and Lewis M. Rutherford, plus two representatives from the U.S. Navy. Great Britain sent a naval captain, an observatory director, a military officer from the Council of India, and Sandford Fleming, as a British representative from Canada.

From the conference's published *Protocol of Proceedings* (1884), one of the first questions facing the delegates was whether the meetings should be open to the general public. The leader of the French delegation, Mr. LeFaivre, was adamant that "nothing could be gained, while the proceedings might be embarrassed or delayed by such a course" (p. 10). He argued that the conference was:

> empowered to confer about matters with which the general public have now nothing to do; that to admit the public to the meetings would destroy their privacy and subject the conference to the influence of an outside pressure which might prove very prejudicial to its proceedings. (p. 20)

The proposal to close the meetings to public view failed in a subsequent vote.

Next, a resolution to invite distinguished scientists to attend and present their views passed after discussion. The French delegates stipulated that the scientists should not vote or initiate discussion. It was clear from their statements that anyone "not authorized by their respective governments" should not "be permitted to influence the decision of this body." The questions to be resolved were "exclusively governmental" (p. 18). Given France's objections to the designation of the Greenwich Observatory by previous scientific conferences, their argument may have been intended to minimize any momentum in favor of the Greenwich meridian.

In spite of the previous consensus by scientific congresses in Venice and Rome, acceptance of the Greenwich meridian was not presumed. Some of the alternative proposals, including Jerusalem, the Great Pyramid, the Azores, and the Bering Strait, which were discussed in previous assemblies, were raised in general discussion and referred to a committee. Two specific alternatives that received general discussion were the possibilities of designating the international meridian either at the Ferro Islands or at a point in the Pacific Ocean at 180 degrees from Greenwich, both of which were introduced by France.

The French objected to Greenwich ostensibly because it was not a neutral site, and because it "cut no great continent, neither Europe nor America" (p. 36). Unless national rivalries could be avoided, they argued, it would be unfair to adopt a universal meridian.

Fleming urged the delegates to "set aside any national or individual prejudices we possess and view the subject as members of one community . . . in fact, as citizens of the world" (p. 75). Great Britain rejected both the Ferro Islands and the point 180 degrees from Greenwich because they did not meet the test of neutrality. The Ferro Islands were considered historically to be French, and the point 180 degrees from Greenwich could not be separated from Greenwich itself, making both of them preferential selections.

France reintroduced the possibility of a reciprocal trade in the discussion when its delegate reviewed the extensive changes in new charts, maps, and atlases that the proposed adoption of Greenwich would require, whereas the English would face no real changes, "leaving to us alone the burden of change" (p. 49). His argument continued:

> When France, at the end of the last century, instituted the metre, did she proceed thus? Did she, as a measure of economy and in order to change nothing in her customs, propose to the world the "Pied de Roi" as a unit of measure? Permit me to say that it is thus a reform should be made and becomes acceptable. It is by setting the example of self-sacrifice; it is by complete self-effacement in any undertaking, that opposition is disarmed and true love of progress is proved. (p. 49)

The French delegate reminded the conference attendees that prior discussions had recognized the inequitable selection of Greenwich and raised the possibility that Great Britain and the United States should adopt the metric system in exchange for France's acquiescence. A Greenwich meridian would be expensive for France in altering its system, but it called for an even greater cost in national pride, conceding to Britain the position of tacit international leader in both shipping and science.

The Spanish representative agreed: "Spain accepts this [metric proposal] in the hope that England and the United States will accept on their part the metric system as she has done herself" (p. 88). The British responded to the French offer to barter the metric system:

> Great Britain has desired that it may be allowed to join the Convention du Metre. . . . Great Britain henceforth will be, as regards its system of weights and measures, exactly in the same position as the United States. In Great Britain the use of metrical weights and measures is authorized by law. . . . It is quite true that the government of England does not hold out any expectation that she will adopt the compulsory use of the metric system, either at the present time, or, so far as that goes, at any future time . . . [the metric system] is an extremely good one and which so far as purely scientific purposes are concerned, is largely in use at the present time. (p. 90)

Whether science should remain ambivalent in this contentious debate was still an open question. A delegate from Brazil said "the arguments which ought to prevail should be, before everything, drawn from science, the only source of truth which alone can enlighten us" (p. 83). The French agreed, asserting the decision where to place the meridian should be based on "exclusively scientific principles" (p. 29). At another time, the French argued "science is absolutely disinterested in the selection. . . . Science appears only as the humble vassal of the powers of the day to consecrate and crown their success" (pp. 91–92).

An unnamed American delegate responded: "From a purely scientific point of view, any meridian can be taken as the prime meridian" (p. 39). William Thomson, an American scientist in attendance at the conference, agreed in principle: "It is the settlement of a question which is a matter of business arrangement. The question is, what will be the most convenient, on the whole, for the whole world. It cannot be said that one meridian is more scientific than another" (p. 94). Lacking any scientific reason to deny the choice, the vote in favor of Greenwich was 22 in favor, 1 against (San Domingo), and 2 abstaining as a matter of protest of the outcome (France and Brazil).

With the outcome of the vote no longer in doubt, a French delegate conceded defeat: "For the present we decline the honor of immolating ourselves alone for progress of a problematic, and eminently secondary order" (p. 94).

Because the United States and Britain refused to acquiesce to the offer to barter the metric system, however disingenuous, the French government subsequently managed to avoid most direct references to Greenwich for the balance of the 19th and the early 20th centuries. France scrupulously defined the international meridian as Paris Mean Time—retarded by 9 min, 21 sec—effectively placing international mean time at Greenwich, without reference to the British location.

The conference considered a series of resolutions to further standardize international time calculations. One rejected proposal would have separated the world's time belts or zones of standard time at 10-min intervals, creating 144 time zones. The conference failed to approve the 24-zone time system, but delegates generally agreed it was the most practical solution (pp. 106–110).

Another proposal considered at the conference regarded the problem of the beginning of the daily cycle. Civilians generally referred to the beginning of a day at midnight, but astronomers and navigators counted days beginning at noon. A proposal initiated at the Rome scientific congress to declare the day begins at noon was rejected. Delegates at the conference agreed that general public acceptance of some time standards was tenuous and the customs of ordinary people should not be challenged. Delegates approved the proposal to begin the so-called universal day at midnight.

Finally, the delegates weighed the problem of how to determine "east" and "west" in a world fully recognized to be spherical. Because the earth rotates in an eastward direction, eastern points ought to precede western points in the time system. The problem they faced, essentially, was what constituted east and west, or where the division between east and west would be placed. Their solution was the demarcation of the "international date line" at the 180th meridian as the easternmost meridian on the globe, "as if the earth were, indeed, flat" (Zerubavel, 1982, p. 16).

The International Meridian Conference failed to adopt the 24-hr clock, which would have dropped the "a.m." and "p.m." designations, but a campaign to adopt the continuous clock was kept alive for at least 5 more years by the U.S. General Time Convention. In spite of strong advocacy by Allen, Fleming, and others, the 24-hr system was never adopted in the United States and Britain except for military use.

CONCLUSION

The innovations that led to international time reform arose from the cumulative changes in 19th-century urbanization and industrialization, and concomitant expansion of international commerce. Scientists set a course leading to mechanization of global time reckoning through innovations of astronomy and shipping. Those innovations were followed by commercially motivated improvements in transportation and cartography, thus global coordination and communication.

Shipping provided the means to carry forward these innovations, not only because of interregional trade contacts between isolated nations, but because ship navigators and astronomers used their technical skills as the cultural imperative of applied science to offer solutions to the cumulative problems in a new urban milieu.

Railroad and telegraphy were important precursors for development of national time systems, but international time reform waited for the maturing of science, accompanied by compelling arguments for the practical needs of a common temporal framework. Scientists could no longer make an explicit claim of neutrality in international time reform, as had Sir George Airy at the British Observatory, in the debate over standardization of international time. In fact, scientists who became engaged in the international dialogue became forerunners of a new communication imperative that spanned national borders.

Still, emergence of a common international meridian was a momentous development both because of the ambivalence of scientists about their political role in government decisions and the diplomatic rivalries between nations like Britain and France. The decision to designate Greenwich as the common meridian was a testament of the uncertain steps that led inevitably to contemporary international cooperation and communication.

ACKNOWLEDGMENTS

I am indebted to research assistants Jeff Orme and Christian Sherwood for their assistance in writing this article.

REFERENCES

Airy, W. (1896). *Authobiography of Sir George Biddell Airy.* London: Cambridge University Press.
Allen, J. S. (1951). *Standard time in America: Why and how it came about and the part taken by the railroads and William Frederick Allen.* New York: Author.
Allen, W. F. (1910). *Short history of standard time and its adoption in North America in 1883.* New York: Author.
Bartky, I. R. (1984). A comment on "The Standardization of Time" by Zerubavel. *American Journal of Sociology, 89,* 1420–1425.
Bartky, I. R. (1985). Inventing, introducing and objecting to standard time. *Vistas in Astronomy, 28,* 105–112.
Bartky, I. R. (1989). The adoption of standard time. *Technology and Culture, 30*(1), 25–56.
Bartky, I. R., & Harrison, E. (1979). Standard and daylight saving time. *Scientific American, 240,* 46–53.
Battaglia, S. A. (1992). Measuring time: Railroads, Taylorism and time consciousness. *Techne: Journal of Technology Studies, 4*(Spring), 34–37.
Beniger, J. R. (1986). *The control revolution: Technological and economic origins of the information society.* Cambridge, MA: Harvard University Press.
Berger, P. L., & Luckmann, T. (1967). *The social construction of reality.* Garden City, NY: Anchor.
Butler, O. (1990). From local to national: Time standardization as a reflection of American culture. In E. Garber (Ed.), *Beyond history of science* (pp. 249–265). Bethlehem, PA: Lehigh University Press.
Carey, J. W. (1989). *Communication as culture: Essays on media and society.* Boston: Unwin Hyman.
Crawford, E. (1992). *Nationalism and internationalism in science, 1880–1939.* Cambridge, England: Cambridge University Press.
Creet, M. (1990). Sandford Fleming and universal time. *Scientia Canadensis, 14,* 66–89.
Dowd, C. F. (1870). *System of national time and its application.* Albany, NY: Weed, Parsons.
Dowd, C. N. (1930). *Charles F. Dowd.* New York: Knickerbocker.
Holbrook, S. H. (1947). *The story of the American railroads.* New York: Crown.
Howse, D. (1980). *Greenwich time.* London: Oxford University Press.
Howse, D. (1997). *Greenwich time and the longitude.* London: Philip Wilson.
Innis, H. (1991). *The bias of communication.* Toronto: University of Toronto Press.
Landes, D. (1983). *Revolution in time: Clocks and the making of the modern world.* Cambridge, MA: Belknap.
Lowe, D. M. (1982). *History of bourgeois perception.* Chicago: University of Chicago Press.
Lyons, F. (1963). *Internationalism in Europe, 1815–1914.* Leyden, The Netherlands: A. W. Sythoff.
Mattelart, A. (2000). *Networking the world: 1794–2000.* Minneapolis: University of Minnesota Press.
Meadows, A. J. (1975). *Greenwich Observatory: Recent history (1836–1975): Vol. 2.* London: Taylor & Francis.
Mumford, L. (1963). *Technics and civilization.* New York: Harcourt, Brace & World.

O'Malley, M. (1990). *Keeping watch: A history of American time.* New York: Viking.
Protocol of Proceedings of International Conference held at Washington for the purpose of fixing a prime meridian and a universal day. (1884). Washington, DC: Gibson Brothers.
Report of the special committee on uniform standard time. (1889). New York: American Society of Civil Engineers.
Smith, H. M. (1976). Greenwich time and the prime meridian. *Vistas in Astronomy, 20,* 219–229.
Stephens, C. (1989). "The most reliable time": William Bond, the New England railroads, and time awareness in 19th-century America. *Technology and Culture, 30*(1), 1–24.
Taylor, G. R., & Neu, I. D. (1956). *The American railroad network, 1861–1890.* Cambridge, MA: Harvard University Press.
Thompson, E. P. (1967). Time, work-discipline, and industrial capitalism, *Past and Present, 38*(December), 56–97.
Thompson, R. L. (1972). *Wiring a continent: The history of the telegraph industry in the United States, 1832–1866.* New York: Arno.
Travis, F. F. (1990). *George Kennan and the American-Russian relationship, 1865–1924.* Athens: Ohio University Press.
Wheeler, G. M. (1885). *Report upon the Third International Geographical Congress and Exhibition at Venice, Italy, 1881.* Washington, DC: U.S. Government Printing Office.
Zerubavel, E. (1982). The standardization of time: A sociohistorical perspective. *American Journal of Sociology, 88*(1), 1–23.

Reading the Russian Revolution: International Communication Research and the Journalism of Lippmann and Merz

Hanno Hardt
Journalism and Mass Communication and Communication Studies
University of Iowa
Faculty of Social Sciences
University of Ljubljana

This article recovers the historical roots of international communication research in the United States from the journalism of Walter Lippmann and Charles Merz. A critical reading of their 1920 study of the New York Times *coverage of the Russian Revolution suggests that their analytically sophisticated presentation of a politically vital topic legitimizes their press criticism as intellectual groundwork for the rise of an international communication research tradition.*

The examination of news as an intellectual exercise inside or outside of academic circles had been firmly established in the United States when media representations of global politics captured public attention by the early 20th century and foreign affairs reporting flourished in the American press.

This article recovers the historical roots of international communication research from the American journalism of the 1920s with a critical reading of one of the earliest and most comprehensive studies of foreign news, the completion of which constitutes an important intellectual marker in the history of the field. The study was concluded in 1920 by Walter Lippmann and Charles Merz, whose insistence on the integrity of the news—which characterized theoretical considerations of journalism at the time—determined their perspective on the relations between the press and its public and informed their own belief in the power of public opinion. This was, after all, a time for Lippmann when "sovereignty had

---

Requests for reprints should be sent to Hanno Hardt, School of Journalism and Mass Communication, University of Iowa, Iowa City, IA 52242. E-mail: hhardt@blue.weeg.uiowa.edu

shifted from the legislature to public opinion," making it necessary for the public "to be assured of accurate, reliable information" (Steel, 1980, p. 172).

Entitled "A Test of the News. An examination of the news reports in the *New York Times* on aspects of the Russian Revolution of special importance to Americans. March 1917–March 1920," the study appeared in a 42-page supplement to the *New Republic* on August 4, 1920 (Lippmann & Merz, 1920). It was most likely the result of a series of controversial reports from Russia by Walter Duranty, a *New York Times* correspondent, whose dispatches were different enough from those of other correspondents to be considered by some the work of a Bolshevik press agent (Salisbury, 1980, pp. 461–463).

Lippmann had joined the *New Republic* in 1914 to participate enthusiastically in the making of a new magazine, whose substance—according to him—would be "American, but sophisticated and critical," while its objective was to "infuse American emotions with American thought" (Steel, 1980, p. 62). Merz had been the Washington correspondent of the *New Republic,* when he changed to the New York *World* in 1919; much later he joined the *New York Times* to eventually become its editorial page director until 1961. Merz wrote "The Voice of a Free Press," a noteworthy editorial (published on January 5, 1956), which became a statement of principle of the *New York Times* in its opposition to the Communist witch hunt of the Congressional Eastland Committee.

Their work remains an extraordinary study, even by today's standards. The authors anticipated not only theoretical and methodological issues of international communication research arising in the 1950s—when numerous content analyses of foreign news coverage in the American press began to compete for attention in a new academic arena of scholarly inquiry—but also their application of a qualitative research design was a precursor of contemporary critical readings of media texts.

Consequently, this article suggests that the roots of a modern history of international communication research may well be traced to an intellectual effort of self-criticism in American journalism. This occurred at a time when the United States became inextricably involved in global affairs and the public's (political) need to know the world turned into a moral responsibility of the press. In addition, a critical reading of Lippmann's and Merz's penetrating public analysis of press practices reveals not only shared interests but also an ideological kinship of journalism and (mass communication) science as value-free practices in their traditional treatment of notions of objectivity.

Moreover, the topic—news coverage of the Russian Revolution—is a particularly important addition to a field of inquiry that would gain in importance with the end of World War II and increased U.S. involvement in foreign affairs, particularly as the Cold War began to affect international relations. After all, how was the emerging Soviet Union, specifically, constructed by the United States, and its press in particular, and what were the predominant images that would surface to characterize the Bolshevik Revolution in Russia after the end of World War I?

The increasing engagement of the United States in foreign affairs at that time was accompanied by extended media attention to political and economic activities abroad. Accordingly, an increasing number of foreign correspondents, foreign bureaus, and foreign news coverage enhanced the traditional purpose of many American newspapers to serve public needs. In the process, they changed from mostly provincial sources of domestic intelligence to cosmopolitan authorities on global affairs, often enough with their own journalists on the world scene, but certainly connected to foreign events through the efforts of U.S. news agencies, like the United Press, International News Service, or the Associated Press, and therefore also to the resources of the *New York Times*.

The field of international and comparative communication studies matured alongside these mounting public demands (including those from government and commerce) for information and explanation, which helped reinforce the international dimension of American mass communication research. Elsewhere I have addressed the ideological foundations of this development (Hardt, 1998); here I want to draw attention to a remarkable early contribution to qualitative international communication research. Rarely cited, hence almost forgotten, the work by Lippmann and Merz (1920) also constitutes a critical reaction to the press coverage of an expanded American presence (or interest) in foreign countries. As such it augments a growing body of academic research into foreign news coverage by U.S. media with a narrative that reinforces the interpretive power of a critical reading reminiscent of contemporary qualitative research methodologies.

Although hardly theorized at the time, the power and influence of the press—as the dominant public medium—and its role in the making of public opinion were widely assumed. Indeed, they had become part of the definition of a modern life that began with urbanization, industrialization, and the spread of large-circulation newspapers around the turn of the 20th century, when the press became more than a detached supplier of information and opinion. Thus, with America's extended involvement in world affairs, there could be no doubt that the nation's media would play a major role in producing the images of people and events that would determine individual and collective judgments (how people thought and felt about each other). The media's (real or imagined) persuasive power, in turn, would also serve specific cultural or political purposes. If contemporary media are the site if not the combatants in a "culture war"—as Hunter (1991) termed it—an earlier press was equally known for its engaged, often partisan struggle over ideologically determined constructions of reality. Indeed, the history of foreign affairs coverage as a reflection of U.S. foreign policy offers an example of the growing interdependence of media and politics in the 20th century. B. C. Cohen (1963) for instance, saw the press as "a political actor of tremendous consequence," able to draw "on its favored position in American political philosophy and on its practical usefulness to foreign policy officials" (p. 268).

Lippmann and Merz (1920) recognized the significance of the Russian Revolution—certainly beyond the impact of immediate events whose newsworthiness was guaranteed by their focus on conflict and armed struggle—as a politically pertinent topic with concrete economic and possibly military consequences for the United States, and therefore, of particular interest to American readers. In fact, the revolutionary struggle in Russia may have been the single most important news event of the first part of the 20th century after the horrors of World War I. Its outcome resulted in an increasingly fierce propaganda campaign of the U.S. government against the ideological foundations of a newly emerging foreign state: the Soviet Union.

Lippmann and Merz (1920) engaged in a systematic, long-term analysis of the *New York Times* news coverage with a close reading of a series of its news reports on diplomatic and military developments that shaped the future of Russia and—by 1920—had determined the fate of the Bolshevik Revolution. By entering into such a long-term study of Russian news coverage, the authors avoided not only the typical limitations of brief, exploratory analyses of specific events, but they were able to reconstruct an ongoing political crisis. With their report in the pages of the *New Republic* they also created a belated opportunity in 1920 for adjusting public opinion about the significance of specific developments in Russia, including the level of credibility regarding the process of news reporting itself. In this sense, their study became a journalistic corrective of a prominent—and what hitherto may have been considered a reliable, if not truthful—rendering of the events in Russia and, therefore, a rare case of press criticism of one of the most important newspapers in the country from within the system.

Their choice of the *New York Times,* according to the authors, suggested its public importance, including its remarkable material capacity to gather, present, and preserve news. They referred to its "means for securing news," its "technically admirable" makeup, the convenience of its index, the accessibility of its "bound volumes," and its prestige as "one of the really great newspapers of the world" (Lippmann & Merz, 1920, p. 1).

The analysis is outstanding for several reasons and constitutes a milestone in the development of international communication research in the United States by directing attention to the consequences of news reporting for the formation of public opinion and to the need for public surveillance of the production of news by the press. By undertaking an analysis of a single, significant newspaper over a considerable period of time, the authors overcame the fragmentation of information, which is inherent in the daily cycle of news production, and reconstructed a holistic account of events, thereby exposing the specific qualities of the news flow. Originally separated by space (or placement) and time (editions), segments of particular events (which lasted over weeks, months, or years) are forged into a coherent, single description.

In the process, the authors introduced (and tested) innovative approaches to the study of news; thus, their critical narrative addresses problems of "truth" or "accuracy," reveals the power of subjectivity and the impact of rhetorical strategies in the construction of news events, and acknowledges the importance of "source credibility." They also described the proximity of news and propaganda and noted the use of specific techniques of representation to reinforce the idea of factual reporting, such as the focus on leaders (strong men), the need for attribution, repetition of facts (deemed important), and selections (or omissions) of facts.

Furthermore, the authors exposed the process of foreign reporting, in general; unlike domestic journalism—which occurs within familiar cultural and social boundaries and is frequently subject to professional or public review and potential adjustment—foreign news gathering not only occurs outside a familiar cultural or social environment, but also lacks opportunities for oversight or review, either by editors and competing journalists or by expert readers as eyewitnesses of specific events. Instead, foreign correspondents—at that time—operated outside the everyday experience of colleagues and readers at home and with the freedom and responsibility that came with reliance on their own professional judgments, expertise, and trust in the editorial process of the respective news organization. On the other hand, intimate acquaintance with interested parties, personal preferences, and reliance on propaganda as fact remained serious threats to the process of reporting, but also to the integrity of information.

But Lippmann and Merz (1920) also responded to a perceived mistrust of news coverage, in general, and particularly of "contentious affairs" (p. 1), if not threats to the integrity of news reporting. They revealed their own belief in the centrality of news in a democratic society and the need for accuracy and reliability, because "a sound public opinion cannot exist without access to the news" (p. 1). Their study is a test of whether the public was denied access to facts. In the process they confronted, albeit implicitly, the rising sensationalism of urban newspapers in the United States, including the popularity of the "yellow press" and the attending fictionalization of the news for the benefit of an increasingly large—and, therefore, important—diversion-seeking reading public.

The question of news is not only a question of fair reporting and disinterested fact, however, but also a question of truth. Lippmann and Merz realized the inherent problem of finding, identifying, and certifying a truthful account of the day's events, especially under adverse external or internal conditions for establishing the nature of specific circumstances. Thus, in a socially and politically complex and shifting situation, the process of reporting is likely to be affected by the tendency to operate from within an identifiable realm of intellectual or political self-interests that obfuscate the boundaries between fact and fiction and help articulate and reinforce the presentation of an ideologically consistent worldview.

Thus, there was no truthful accounting of the situation in Russia, according to the authors, and there could be no authoritative reports when "able and disinterested observers furnish contradictory evidence out of which no objective criteria emerge" (Lippmann & Merz, 1920, p. 2). Consequently, the notion of accuracy, or truth, becomes a relative concept, plagued by the inability to reproduce a reliable measure, and, therefore, turns out to be less useful for determining quality in news reporting than the notion of reliability. The latter concept suggests yet another standard of observation, the strength of which lies in the availability of sufficient, consensually undisputed details of specific incidents. Their discussion contains an implicit acknowledgment of the difficulty to believe in the ability (or willingness) of the press to reproduce reality or a universal truth despite the commonsense belief that the press is a mirror of society and reflects—or ought to reflect—the way things are.

Thus, the authors resorted to a different standard of measurement by announcing that the "reliability of the news is tested in this study by a few definite and decisive happenings about which there is no dispute" (Lippmann & Merz, 1920, p. 2). This is a way of establishing "truth" by expert consensus, as the construction of events now rests on the reliability of shared observations. Lippmann and Merz (1920) reduced their inquiry to one major question:

> Whether the reader of the news was given a picture of various phases of the revolution which survived the test of events, or whether, he was misled into believing that the outcome of events would be radically different from the actual outcome. (p. 2)

Consequently, a series of specific episodes in the history of the Russian Revolution emerged to constitute the testing ground of the *New York Times* news coverage. These incidents ranged from the failure of the Russian army offensive (under Kerensky) in July 1917, the overthrow of the Provisional Government by the Soviets in November 1917 and their separate peace with Germany in March 1918, and the failures of various military campaigns (by Kolchak, Denikin, and Yudenitch), to the continuing existence of the Soviet government by March 1920. They are confirmed episodes that were examined by the authors in 12 chapters, beginning with the July offensive in 1917 and ending with the failure of international intervention in 1920.

The critical reading of pertinent articles in the pages of the *New York Times* against standards of reliability also includes the use of two superimposed, comparative maps to illustrate distances and effectively project the size of the United States onto the vastness of Russia (e.g., "Kolchak's retreat from Perm to Irkutsk was accordingly a retreat corresponding to one from Santa Fe, N. M. to a point off the Bahama Islands"; Lippmann & Merz, 1920, p. 25). The visualization of the physical context not only familiarizes the reader with the territories in the news, but also reinforces the extent of the problem of providing a reliable accounting of the political and military shifts of power in a nation of enormous proportions and, thus, adds to an understanding of the emerging narrative in the *New Republic*.

Although the Russia of the aftermath of World War I was a faraway place for most Americans, Lippmann and Merz (1920) suggested that readers needed to know about the specific issues of the day, and "whether the Red regime was tottering to its fall or marching to the military conquest of the world," because on any of these questions "depended some aspect of policy involving lives, trade, finance, and national honor" (p. 2). The latter observation is also a reminder of the ethnocentric nature of American news, which dictates news values and priorities for covering foreign affairs. News must be relevant, and it is relevant only when it contains a "local" angle. The result is a form of objective professional judgment—beyond the potential interests of readers in particular social or political issues regarding the domestic affairs (of Russia)—which guides the approach to news gathering and directs editorial decision making. The consequences of ignoring such a narrow perspective (on what is relevant or not in the presentation of news) by perpetuating the climate of opinions and political speculations instead may have contributed to the authors' ultimate conclusion about the *New York Times* coverage; they suggested that: "From the point of view of professional journalism the reporting of the Russian Revolution is nothing short of a disaster. On the essential questions the net effect was always misleading, and misleading news is worse than none at all" (p. 3).

Lippmann and Merz (1920) were particularly concerned about the implications for the future of the press in the democratic process of sharing relevant information, when:

> a great people in a supreme crisis could not secure the minimum of necessary information on a supremely important event. When that truth has burned itself into men's consciousness, they will examine the news in regard to other events, and begin a searching inquiry into the sources of public opinion. (p. 3)

Their judgment was harsh, and they demanded that the "indispensable preliminary to a fundamental task of the Twentieth Century" be: "the insurance to a free people of such a supply of news that a free government can be successfully administered" (p. 3). The press, and particularly influential, prestigious newspapers like the *New York Times,* must be held to the highest standards of performance, not only because "the reliability of the news is the premise on which democracy proceeds," but also because a "great newspaper is a public service institution" (p. 3), with responsibilities that equal those of schools, churches, or government organizations.

These are stringent requirements that reflect not only the authors' belief in the strict separation of information and opinion, but also confirm their insistence on the centrality of the press in the political process: Freedom of the press alone is not a sufficient guarantee for the reliability or accuracy of facts; responsible practice in the interest of advancing the common good remains equally important. Yet, as Lippmann (1915/1982) observed several years earlier, the reporting of international affairs often ends in a "'strong' stand" that is "least dangerous" and "produces an exhilarating sense of importance," whereas a "'weak' stand" is "a costly and thankless task for an editor" and an appeal to "thought which is pale rather than to lusts which are strong" (p. 399).

Their close reading of the *New York Times* over a 3-year period anticipated a specific, indisputable level of knowledge among readers about specific events of the Russian Revolution as an objective measure, tempered by varying levels of interest or sophistication that mark any reading of the news. For instance, they distinguished between levels of interpretation by referring to the habits of "trained" and "casual" readers; the former encounter "obscurely placed dispatches" and read "between the lines of the other dispatches," whereas the latter concentrate on "captions or prominent news" (Lippmann & Merz, 1920, pp. 4–6). Consequently, Lippmann and Merz accounted not only for the qualitative differences among a reading public—while anticipating contemporary issues of media literacy—but they also indicated (and assured their own readers of) the diligence of their own reading and the depth of their engagement with the pertinent news accounts of their study. Their references to qualitatively different information-seeking techniques or habits allow for a differentiated appraisal of the uses of newspapers, including the *New York Times*, and avoid the potential blindspots of a standardized or one-sided, expert reading of the news. They also raised (unanswered) questions about (the acquisition of) communicative competence and the ability of readers to participate in the interpretation of news.

Their "quantitative" measure consisted of dividing the *New York Times* news coverage into "optimistic" and "pessimistic" accounts of events—either from the point of view of the Russian government or the Soviet side. The result is a simple, yet effective assessment of the coverage, based on the tendency or flavor of the reporting. Accordingly, they asked, "did the news lead to correct or incorrect expectations" regarding either the "morale and strength of Russia's armies" during the early months of the conflict (Lippmann & Merz, 1920, p. 4) or "the stability of the Bolshevik regime" (p. 10) at a later date?

Lippmann and Merz (1920) concluded that time and again the "values placed upon news items were wrong, wrong by the ultimate test of battle" (p. 5), and they suggested specifically that "the news as a whole is dominated by the hopes of the men who composed the news organization" (p. 3) and that the "news about Russia is a case of seeing not what was, but what men wanted to see" (p. 3). In fact, this insight may be the most important finding of the study, because it exposes the nature of journalistic objectivity: unattainable by working journalists acting on their own understanding of the world and mythical for purposes of a critical discourse about the press and society. The resulting observations about the quality of reporting imply fairness, balance, and common sense as objective standards and reflect on ignorance, naiveté, or improper intent as poorly applied subjectivity. Thus, the authors flatly stated that the "chief censor and the chief propagandist were hope and fear in the minds of reporters and editors" who wanted to "win the war" and "ward off bolshevism" (p. 3).

Lippmann and Merz (1920) moved the issue of subjectivity (and intent) into the center of their investigation; by examining the process of news production, including the presentation of manufactured facts, they threw light on the hidden motives of journalists (and editors) and problematized the business of news coverage in general. In this case, specifically, to win the war and defeat bolshevism became the ultimate goals of "enterprising men" who submitted to "objective censorship and propaganda" in the conduct of their professional duties. The notion of subjectivity was defined as a betrayal of the "free pursuit of facts" and characterized as the uncritical and, therefore, unprofessional acceptance of unreliable sources and suspicious accounts, the net result of "boundless credulity, and an untiring readiness to be gulled, and on many occasions with a downright lack of common sense" (p. 3).

These observations introduced the idea of objectivity—the impact of which was subsequently reflected in interpretive writings about American journalism by Schudson (1978) or Schiller (1981), among others—also as a major social science concern of mass communication research during the next decades. At the same time, Lippmann and Merz revealed the ideological nature of their own critical expectations. Indeed, Lippmann (1931, pp. 433–441) continued to argue much later that only objectivity makes for good journalism. Consequently, their understanding of objectivity as a journalistic imperative rests on a belief in reality as a world of facts that can be recovered and reported by journalists, who are able to rise above ideological differences, political preferences, and cultural (or personal) biases to "re-present" the events of the day. As such, their understanding reinforced a technical rationality that ruled social thought and cultural performances, including the work of journalists, and offered a fitting response, at that particular historical moment, to an increasingly industrialized public mind. Objectivity as a professional expectation continued to dominate the idea of American journalism for some years to follow.

Lippmann and Merz (1920) provided extensive explanations of the type and quality of news that was generated by the *New York Times* in pursuit of political goals. They documented and described the mechanisms of censorship and propaganda that came to shape the reproduction of Russia and its revolutionary struggle on the pages of the newspaper. They also listed the sources of these practices, which were revealed in the bias of special interest groups or institutions and their own creation of the political or military realities of Russia at the time. They included not only the use of questionable news sources (and ready-made reports), but also strategies of repetition of specific sets of facts. The result was the exposure of a specific bias (toward an optimistic view of the issues) and the confirmation of the spread of propaganda, which casts doubt on the process of reporting and diminishes one of its central characteristics, trustworthiness. The authors concluded that "Insistently appearing in the news, the steady repetition in these reports left its inevitable impression on the reader," and they asked, "How trustworthy were the sources from which this material was drawn?" (p. 11). In doing so, the authors also addressed the issue of "source credibility," a concept of later

U.S. mass communication research, with their revelations of untrustworthy (or biased) sources. They also documented the use of corrupted, sometimes semiofficial sources with hardly a measure of authority to create a picture of Russia that proved to be misleading. Specifically, the "reliance upon unidentified 'experts' and 'diplomats' and upon 'official quarters' where rumor invariably finds its favorite haven, particularly with the subordinate, these sources represent in fact a fairly irresponsible assortment" (pp. 40–41).

Also, repetition as a method of influencing public opinion became a frequent enough occurrence in the *New York Times* coverage to raise suspicion among readers. In noting some incidents of repetition, for instance, Lippmann and Merz (1920) reported:

> Thirty different times the power of the Soviets was definitely described as being on the wane. Twenty times there was news of a serious counter-revolutionary menace. Five times was the explicit statement made that the regime was certain to collapse. And fourteen times that collapse was said to be in progress. Four times Lenin and Trotzky [sic] were planning flight. Three times they had already fled. Five times the Soviets were "tottering." Three times their fall was "imminent," . . . twice Lenin planned retirement; once he had been killed; and three times he was thrown in prison. (pp. 10–11)

The stability of the Bolshevik regime had obvious political consequences for the U.S. government and Western (European) diplomacy. A repetition of optimistic accounts about its collapse, however, eventually became a "suspicious fact" among sophisticated readers; Lippmann and Merz (1920) suggested that reiteration may create doubt and lead to opposite conclusions, as casual readers may be lulled into complacency. They indicated the inherent difficulties of absorbing the news, especially of complicated, foreign issues, even for the trained reader, and even more so when disreputable sources and subjective agendas of news organizations and their representatives contaminate the relations between the press as a public service and readers in need of reliable information. At the same time, the authors rejected ideas about any organized attempts to propagandize readers of the *New York Times,* but concluded that the "difficulties revealed are professional; where the news is misleading in the net effect it is because the emphasis has been misplaced by the powerful passions of the war" (p. 13). In this sense, reporting the news becomes a struggle between (personal) passion and objective (or fair) observation.

On the other hand, Lippmann and Merz (1920) agreed that the *New York Times* engaged in open support of military intervention with "a vast amount of news directly advocating or directly forecasting the desired intervention." They asserted "that the news columns in this period were used to persuade the readers of the wisdom of a certain policy, held by the *Times* itself, will hardly be disputed" and concluded that the news had been invaded by editorial opinions; moreover, they asserted that "a great deal of the news about Russia in the period under consideration was marked by such propagandistic methods" (pp. 15–16).

An example was provided by the appearance of the "Red Peril" in the news accounts of the *New York Times* throughout this period, starting right after the armistice; at that time, the Red Peril played a part in turning Allied diplomacy from peace, only to return in 1920, when the Bolshevik Revolution seemed to have succeeded, to "cast its shadow on the sky" (Lippmann & Merz, 1920, p. 38). Lippmann and Merz recorded a "long train . . . picturing the Red Peril" and touching on several themes related to its effects on the rest of the world. They "gauge the effect of steady repetition" during 1 month (January 1920) and noted the regular visits on the activities of the Red Peril by *New York Times* coverage. Accordingly, the bolshevist menace threatened the Middle East, the Baltic states, India, Europe, Mesopotamia and Persia, Poland, Eastern and Southern Asia, Azerbaijan and Georgia, and the Caucasus. The authors concluded that the "net effect" of this series of (14) dispatches

> was certainly towards checking growth of an opinion that Russia's failure to rally to the interventionists had demonstrated the need of a new policy—of considering the Soviets an authority with which some sort of truce could and must be made. You cannot make truce with Peril. (p. 40)

Beyond the impact of this specific propagandistic practice of *New York Times* journalism in 1920, the designation of the Soviet Union as the "Red Peril" marks the beginning of a 70-year-long propaganda campaign with phrases that range from the post-World War I threats of the "Bolshevist menace" to Ronald Reagan's 1980s warnings about the "evil empire." The escalating vocabulary of mistrust and hatred became the most reliable ammunition in the propaganda arsenal of the United States and was freely used by the media to keep the "red scare" alive, if only as a media event. Thus, even in the 1920s Lippmann and Merz (1920) were able to observe that the Red Peril "appeared at every turn to obstruct the restoration of peace in Eastern Europe and Asia, and to frustrate the resumption of economic life," and they concluded that "with armed intervention no longer a possibility, it was the propaganda in the news" (p. 41).

Although the authors were quick to suggest that they had "proceeded without animus against the *Times,* and with much admiration for its many excellent qualities" (Lippmann & Merz, 1920, p. 3), they provided little evidence of these qualities beyond those mentioned in connection with their choice of the newspaper as an object of their examination. Instead, their analysis, "a piece of inductive evidence on the problem of the news" (p. 4), suggests a dereliction of the "supreme duties" because the *New York Times* failed to "supply the information on which public opinion feeds," resulting in "disastrous" coverage of the Russian Revolution (p. 3).

Lippmann and Merz (1920) realized that constructing the Russian Revolution had to remain a creative effort, subject to the visions and experiences of the journalist as expert storyteller; complex situations require a skillful immersion in the conditions of the time. In fact, they conceded that "reporting is one of the most difficult professions, requiring much expert knowledge and serious education," and a lack of adequate preparation results in "improperly trained men (having) seriously misled a whole nation." An unsuspecting public with high expectations of the *New York Times* as a trustworthy news source did not think twice about its choice. Thus, it is "habit rather than preference which makes readers accept news from correspondents whose usefulness is about that of an astrologer or alchemist" (p. 42).

As a result of their investigation, Lippmann and Merz (1920) came to believe "that the professional standards of journalism are not high enough, and the discipline by which standards are maintained not strong enough, to carry the press triumphantly through a test so severe as that provided by the Russian Revolution" (p. 41). These standards were violated by relying on official, semiofficial, or even anonymous statements of opinion as facts, by depending on untrustworthy journalists, because their "sympathies are too deeply engaged" (pp. 41–42), by inadequate preparation of correspondents, and by the breakdown of "the time honored tradition of protecting news against editorials" (p. 42).

The authors lamented the absence of journalistic standards, yet because their critique focuses on the profession rather than on the corporate power of the press as a commercial concern—or on the public practices of acquiring opinions—it fails to address the more complicated relationship between professional conduct and institutional interests; that is, compliance with specific commercial or political goals at the expense of professional freedom. About 80 years later, the activities of the press—and its position in society—are still met with suspicion and lack of respect, whereas the standards of journalism are rapidly changing to embrace the interests of commerce, and consumers replace the traditional notions of the "public" as a matter of fact.

Lippmann and Merz may have been skeptical themselves at the time about any radical departure from traditional ways of doing journalism in America and return to a collective, democratically inspired approach to improving the profession. Given their ideological or philosophical bent, they wanted to rely on the public and called on public interest to address the shortcomings of the press and to help raise expectations about its performance as a public service institution. Implicit in their suggestions of public criticism—which seemed to have had no immediate effect—are much later developments, however, like the establishment of press councils, or more recently, the institution of public journalism with its cooperative dimension and involvement of the public in directing the production of news.

Nevertheless, "A Test of the News" is an early exercise in critical media studies and a significant contribution to international communication research, because of its extensive treatment of a major 20th-century phenomenon: the role of the press (to be followed soon by broadcasting, film, and television) in the construction of global realities and the public's need to know international developments for the purpose of domestic decision making in politics and commerce. In the process, Lippmann and Merz articulated not only a qualitative methodology to cope with the demands of a critical reading, but they also identified a number of issues that would surface in later studies of international communication and mass communication research. Moreover, their work is filled with ideas that fit well into an emerging tradition of critical communication studies and its recognition of the necessary relationship between democracy and communication.

Lippmann and Merz may not have been aware of their long-term contributions to communication research at the time, when they took on America's most famous and internationally respected newspaper over a subject matter of major consequence for the life of the republic during the rest of the 20th century. But in doing so, they also made an impressive contribution to investigative journalism, and their analysis is an appropriate reminder of the close relationship between the practices of the social sciences and journalism. Both represent a distinguished tradition of intellectual labor in Western societies—as noted by Weber (1918/1946)—that celebrates the labor of political journalism and concludes at about the same time that "a really good journalistic accomplishment requires at least as much 'genius' (*Geist*) as any scholarly accomplishment" (p. 96).

Lippmann and Merz (1920) did not confine their analysis to the performance of the *New York Times,* but began to raise questions about professional standards that address the status of 1920s journalism and the production of news, in particular. With remarkable clarity and directness, the authors privileged the process of reporting and suggested not only its inherent difficulty, but stressed the need for expert knowledge and "serious" education among those deployed to cover international politics, wars, or commerce. Their demand for the protection of news against editorial interests is a clear call for recognizing the integrity of reporters and their work of shaping worldviews and may have reflected their own experiences—and expectations—as journalists.

Thus, the authors revealed that the fight against international communism began with a violation of basic journalistic standards and against public expectations regarding the output of reliable information by the (allegedly) most reliable source of intelligence, the *New York Times.* Their findings invite contemporary speculations about the cumulative effects of 70 years of propaganda against the Soviet Union—produced by the American media—beginning with this specific example of a partisan, journalistic rendition of anti-Communist rhetoric. Their study also suggests the dangers of private ownership without public responsibility and documents the ease with which personal or institutional judgments could (and most likely did) prevail throughout this period. The result is a deliberately constructed vision of the "enemy"—the creation of "pictures in our heads" (1922, pp. 3–20), to use Lippmann's famous phrase—that may have had a major and long-lasting effect on more recent public sentiments regarding U.S. Cold War policies.

The study is also a substantive prelude to Lippmann's extensive and increasingly pessimistic reflections on the public, public opinion, and the workings of the press in a democratic society. They would appear later in a series of books, including *Liberty and the News* (1920), *Public Opinion* (1922), and *The Phantom Public* (1925); these works problematize the making of public opinion beyond the role of the press (and its editorial practices) and chronicle the fate of the individual in an increasingly complex environment and the rise of expert opinion as knowledge about a world whose image depends more and more on the work of the media. His book-length treatises on the press—together with this study of Russian news—continue to serve as reminders of the need to question journalistic practices and to engage in the surveillance of media constructions of the social and political realities of our own days habitually and with determination while exploring further the ways in which the public forms its opinions and participates in the democratic process.

"A Test of the News" documents the encounter of 1920s American journalism with subjectivity, bias, self-interest, and the predicament of private enterprise without public responsibility. It is also a prominent cultural, ideological critique, which suggests to the contemporary reader the peculiar contradictions between the ideals of an optimistic, progressive age and the concrete historical conditions of contemporary democratic practices, when an understanding of public communication turns from participation to privilege. In this sense, the study not only confirms the power of the press, but also reminds its readers of the consequences of a self-seeking journalism of special interests, when freedom of the press turns from its emancipatory potential into a private privilege to become a source of deception and mistrust and undermines public confidence in the role of journalism. Eighty years later, the contemporary reporting on Russia is yet another case in point. According to S. C. Cohen (2000), the recent "US media narrative of post-Communist Russia was manichean and based largely on accounts propounded by US officials" (p. 24). It contains nothing about the real economic and social conditions of the Russian people, but continues to celebrate a failed economic policy amid widespread corruption and outright theft.

As a constitutive element in the history of international communication research in the United States, this study of the *New York Times* suggests the analytical potential of self-criticism as a cultural practice of the journalism of the day; it also substantiates the ideological proximity of journalism and science in concerns about producing an objective representation of the world. The critical journalism of Lippmann and Merz (1920) demonstrates the contiguousness of a critical narrative across professional boundaries and confirms the role of modern media in the construction of (political) realities. As a critical, intellectual project, their work marks the beginnings of a large number of inquiries into

East–West relations, the "threats" of communism, and the state of the Cold War in media reports throughout the remainder of the 20th century. Their efforts also illustrate the success of applying high intellectual standards and expert knowledge to a critical study of international news, including the uses of political history (of Russia and the United States) and cultural practices (of journalism) as necessary contexts for explaining a potentially complex relationship between presenting and reading the news under specific political circumstances. The result is an analytically sophisticated presentation of a politically vital topic with conclusions—more than 80 years later—that may still inspire a broader and more inclusive investigation of the role of the American media in the construction of the Soviet Union as a military threat to global peace and of communism as an ideology of world conflict during a major part of the 20th century.

REFERENCES

Cohen, B. C. (1963). *The press and foreign policy.* Princeton, NJ: Princeton University Press.
Cohen, S. C. (2000). American journalism and Russia's tragedy. *The Nation, 271*(9), 23–30.
Hardt, H. (1998). The world according to America: Ideology and comparative media studies. In *Interactions: Critical studies in communication, media, and journalism* (pp. 137–154) Boulder, CO: Rowman & Littlefield.
Hunter, J. D. (1991). *Culture wars.* New York: Basic Books.
Lippmann, W. (1920). *Liberty and the news.* New York: Macmillan.
Lippmann, W. (1922). *Public opinion.* New York: Macmillan.
Lippmann, W. (1925). *The phantom public.* New York: Harcourt Brace.
Lippmann, W. (1931, March). Two revolutions in the American press. *Yale Review,* pp. 433–441.
Lippmann, W. (1982). Some notes on the press. In C. Rossiter & J. Lane (Eds.), *The essential Lippmann: A political philosophy for liberal democracy* (pp. 398–399). Cambridge, MA: Harvard University Press. (Original work published 1915)
Lippmann, W., & Merz, C. (1920). A test of the news. *The New Republic, 23*(296), 1–42.
Salisbury, H. E. (1980). *Without fear or favor: An uncompromising look at the New York Times.* New York: Ballantine.
Schiller, D. (1981). *Objectivity and the news: The public and the rise of commercial journalism.* Philadelphia: University of Pennsylvania Press.
Schudson, M. (1978). *Discovering the news: A social history of American newspapers.* New York: Basic Books.
Steel, R. (1980). *Walter Lippmann and the American century.* New York: Random House.
Weber, M. (1946). Politics as a profession. In H. H. Gerth & C. W. Mills (Eds.), *From Max Weber: Essays in sociology* (pp. 77–128). New York: Oxford University Press. (Original work published 1918)

Beyond the Four Theories of the Press: A New Model of National Media Systems

Jennifer Ostini
Sydney, Australia

Anthony Y. H. Fung
School of Journalism and Communication
The Chinese University of Hong Kong

Work on categorization of national press systems in the last 40 years has been grounded in the well-known Four Theories of the Press. Whereas this approach has been strongly criticized by international scholars for its idealism and its poverty of empiricism, it is still widely taught in introductory journalism courses across the country, and few theorists have engaged in grounding the theory with data in international settings. Although journalism is contextualized and constrained by press structure and state policies, it is also a relatively autonomous cultural production of journalists negotiating between their professionalism and state control. This article thus proposes a new model incorporating the autonomy of individual journalistic practices into political and social structural factors—the interaction of which might currently more accurately represent press practices in the new international order. With an understanding of the background of the journalistic practices and state policies of 4 countries/cities, the multinational media coverage of a specific event is explicated in the light of the new model. This new model explains the journalistic variations that cannot be clearly revealed using a state-policy press model alone.

The world order has changed greatly in the last decade. As people celebrate the fall of communism and the hope of a new millennium, it seems that few have pondered how we can reinterpret our social, media, and information orders

---

Requests for reprints should be sent to Anthony Y. H. Fung, School of Journalism and Communication, The Chinese University of Hong Kong, Shatin, NT, Hong Kong. E-mail: anthonyfung@cuhk.edu.hk

using new theories and frameworks. Many of the old frameworks—including those of the media such as the Four Theories of the Press (Four Theories)—are obsolete and inapplicable for contemporary analysis. The new order has already annulled their explanatory power. We need new ideas to account for the development of our internationalized and diverse forms of media. Such theoretical models must go beyond the state-policy and normative focus of the Four Theories as a conception of "what the press should be and do" (Siebert, Peterson, & Schramm, 1956). Theoretical models should not be bounded by dominant ideological perspectives and hinged on certain historical blocs—namely those of Communism and the Cold War—and subsequently void with the demise of these concepts. Postulating a model of media systems that will survive the test of history and empiricism, as well as sufficiently explaining the new order is an important concern.

The purpose of this article is twofold. Previous constructions and conceptions of media models are reviewed and an attempt is made to develop a new model to account for the global media systems. Following this, ideas are suggested for ways to test this media model based on content analysis of multinational media coverage of a specific event.

A BRIEF HISTORICAL REVIEW OF MEDIA MODELS

The Four Theories of the Press

The Four Theories are a linear combination of two analytical subdimensions based on state systems: authoritarian and libertarian. Siebert (1956) referred to the authoritarian dimension as the original prototype and most pervasive of all the dimensions. By this, he meant that this dimension continues to influence press practices even when a government may officially subscribe to other systems. This assumes, from a structural-functionalist perspective, that the state has a fundamental interest in maintenance and stability of the power structure in its favor. In this model, libertarian theory is held to be the ideal in which the prime function of society is to advance the interests of its individual members (Siebert et al., 1956, p. 40). Adherence to libertarian ideals involves an innate distrust of the role of government and the state. State surveillance becomes the basic social function of media (Wright, 1986). The Soviet Communist model is seen as an extreme application of authoritarian ideas—in that media are totally subordinated to the interests and functions of the state. The social responsibility model is based on the idea that media have a moral obligation to society to provide adequate information for citizens to make informed decisions. In contrast, libertarian theory argues that the "citizen . . . had the right to be uninformed or misinformed, but the tacit assumption was that his rationality and his desire for truth would keep him from being so" (Siebert et al., 1956, p. 101).

Revisions of the Four Theories

The Importance of Political Economy

Lowenstein (Merrill & Lowenstein, 1971/1979) argued that the original Four Theories lacked the requisite flexibility to analyze modern press systems and expanded it into Five Theories by adding a category based on ownership. To more appropriately depict the political situation at the time, he renamed the Soviet Communist model as the social-centralist model in the 1971 edition of his book and further named it as social-authoritarian in the second edition. By using the term *social-authoritarian,* his model removes the negative connotations of the Communist label and replaces it with a concept linking it to the social responsibility theory. The social responsibility theory was relabeled social-libertarian as a derivation from the libertarian theory. The concept of social centrist in which a government or the public owned press sources to ensure the operational spirit of the libertarian philosophy was used to describe the new fifth category (Merrill & Lowenstein, 1971/1979, p. 164).

The addition of this fifth element based on the level of ownership allowed for categorization of press systems based on private, multiparty, or government ownership. However, it failed to either explain variance or add more analytical power to the existing categories. The original Four Theories were based on ownership of the press as well as functions and thus, Lowenstein's explicit labeling of ownership categories seems superfluous.

Hachten (1981, p. 61) also proposed five theories or concepts of the press emphasizing politics and economics: authoritarian, Western, Communist, revolutionary, and developmental or third world. Hachten's conception of authoritarianism was similar to that of Siebert et al. (1956) and Lowenstein (Merrill & Lowenstein, 1971/1979). However, his Western concept encompassed both the libertarian and social-responsibility models with its defining characteristic being that it is relatively free of arbitrary government controls (Hachten, 1981, p. 64). Under the Communist concept, media are tools that serve as implements of revelation (by revealing purposes and goals of party leaders) as well as instruments of unity and consensus (p. 67). The main difference between authoritarian and Communist systems is ownership. In authoritarian systems, press can be privately owned as opposed to state ownership in Communist systems. Hachten defined the revolutionary concept as being illegal and subversive mass communication utilizing the press and broadcasting to overthrow a government or wrest control from alien rulers (pp. 69–70). He admitted that examples of this type of press are difficult to find and suggested only the example of underground presses in Nazi-occupied France (p. 70).

Finally, the developmental model was seen to have arisen out of a combination of Communist ideas, anti-Americanism, and social-responsibility ideals (Hachten, 1981, p. 72). Hachten saw the defining characteristic of this concept as being the idea that individual rights must be subordinated to the larger goals of nation-building and thus must support authority. This concept is also seen to be a negative response to the Western model. However, Hachten's classification never yields a clear distinction of the press systems, for the analytical dimensions are defined both under the system of the state (authoritarian, Western, Communist) and the functions of the media (revolutionary and developmental).

Akhavan-Majid and Wolf (1991) argued that the fundamental flaw of the original Four Theories was that it ignored the role of economic influence in media systems. They argued that a number of factors have resulted, not in deviation from the libertarian norm in the United States, but in fundamental changes to the structure of U.S. media for which a new explanatory model must be found. These factors include increasing concentration and conglomeration of ownership and the subordination of the ideals of diversity and independence to the corporate search for synergy and profits (Akhavan-Majid & Wolf, 1991, p. 139). Instead of the libertarian model as an explanation for U.S. media systems, Akhavan-Majid and Wolf suggested an elite power group model that is seen as the opposite of the libertarian model. The main reason for this is that U.S. media are characterized as having concentration in media outlets, integration with other elite power groups (such as big business and government elite), and two-way flow of influence and control between the government and the press (p. 142). These characteristics of media are argued to result in decreasing diversity of opinions and representations and a lessening of the media's watchdog role.

Idealism and Press Theories

Many of these theories have reflected Western idealism and championship of a Western perspective of democracy. The work of Picard (1985) is no exception. He reviewed previous categories of state–press relations and added a further concept, that of the democratic socialist theory of the press. This theory argued that the press's purposes are to provide an avenue for expression of public views and to fuel the political and social debates necessary for the continued development of democratic governance (p. 67). Under the umbrella of the theory, the role of the state is to ensure the ability of citizens to use the press and to preserve and promote media plurality (p. 67). Akhavan-Majid and Wolf (1991, p. 141) presented Picard's model as one that attempts to prescribe a means of restoring the essential democratic-libertarian elements (i.e., diversity, plurality, and public access and participation) to the U.S. mass media system. Picard argued that the fundamental difference between this and other theories is that the democratic socialist theory regards media as public utilities rather than tools of the state or privately owned institutions. However, he subsumed democratic socialist, social responsibility, and libertarian ideas under Western theory.

Balancing Structural Control and Individual Responsibility

Altschull (1984/1995) moved further away from the Four Theories. Although unwilling to dogmatically categorize media types and trying to avoid the fallacy that the groupings are mutually exclusive or collectively exhaustive, he identified three categories: market, communitarian, and advancing (p. 419). In simplest and idealized terms, market systems operate with no outside interference—as documentors of society, not as agents of change. Communitarian systems serve the people by reflecting the desires of a political party or government, but are not themselves agents of change. In advancing systems media serve as partners of government (p. 426). In Altschull's typology, all media systems seek truth and try to be socially responsible. Only in market systems are the media seen as having no role in political and cultural education. All systems seek to serve the people but in different ways. The market system focuses on impartiality while actually supporting capitalism. Communitarian systems serve by trying to modify opinions to support correct doctrine (p. 429) and advancing systems try to promote beneficial change and peace. Altschull (p. 427) made a significant contribution in identifying beliefs about media systems as articles of faith that are irrational, not arrived at by reason, often held with the passion shown by true believers. Thus, many conflicts (especially at international levels) cannot be solved because they are clashes of faith rather than reason.

Limits of Previous Models

The fundamental problem with many of the media models discussed here is the prescription that these authors attempt to impose on current systems—that is, they try to prescribe rather than to describe social phenomena by using an empirical basis for inquiry. Theories of the press from Siebert et al. (1956) onward have focused on normative theories largely based on traditional mass media structures. Normative theories lack explanatory power in that they are based on how things should be and do not necessarily relate to how things are. As discussed earlier, the original Four Theories model was constrained by the ideology and historical circumstances of its inception. Political changes in the world have limited the explanatory power of the model. For example, the Soviet Union no longer exists and socialism in China is very different from Cold War ideas about Communism.

In addition, the Four Theories model (developed in a Western setting) assumed an evolutionary mode of development in which press systems would move from Communist to authoritarian to liberalism and on to social responsibility. This assumption has proved to be false and this one-way, linear, and somewhat ethnocentric epistemology undermines the basis of the model. Subsequent models based on the same, or similar, assumptions such as Hachten's (1981) political development model, have similar difficulties.

Picard's (1985) model illustrates the problem of focusing exclusively on state–press relationships. This approach ignores dynamic microlevel interaction among organizations, journalists, and the state. Akhavan-Majid and Wolf (1991) provided the vital missing element of economics to the model but again operated at a macro rather than a micro level of analysis. Consideration of media economics is vital to understanding press systems but media operations, journalistic reporting, and editorial decisions are not totally determined by the economic base (of capitalists and the state; Williams, 1977). A primary focus on the economy and the state ignores the semiautonomous nature of the press that operates also on the basis of journalistic professionalism. On the other hand, taking a neo-marxist approach, the press economy should be analyzed in the "first instance," not in the last analysis (Hall, 1982). According to this critique, analysis of the state and the economy remains an important first step, but should not be the ultimate purpose of the study. In an analysis of the political economy of the press, Murdoch (1982) hinted at the possibility of integrating both the "intentional model" and "structural models" (pp. 118–150). The Four Theories of the press focuses exclusively on structural factors and ignores the individual journalist's autonomy, professionalism, and enduring values. Primary focus on traditional mass media also excludes new media types and changing forms of traditional media (McQuail, 1994).

The question is whether a new model can be constructed that bridges structural factors and professional practice while allowing for the incorporation of new media forms and structures and can be empirically tested. This article seeks to present such a new model and to illustrate the model's potential through a preliminary case study of press coverage of a specific event.

TOWARD A NEW PRESS MODEL

Structural Factors

As with previous models, the main structural factor that will be taken into account is the system of government with its economic, political, and cultural subsystems. Different political systems are typically generically labeled as capitalist or socialist, democratic or authoritarian. These generalized labels do not take into account variants of socialism as economic structures tied closely to public policy and political arrangements of government, nor democracy laden with its values of capitalism and profit orientation.

In this model, the structural constraints imposed on the press and journalists are represented (as suggested in many other models) as one dimension: one end of the scale labeled as democracy and the other, authoritarianism. Democracy is simply defined in the context of media as being political freedom for the media to freely criticize state policies and to operate largely without government controls in a free marketplace of ideas without precluding the possibility of invisible control of the market. Authoritarianism is defined as a system that enforces strict obedience by the media to political authorities. Constraints may be political and economic. In the context of media, authoritarianism is operationalized as strict control of content by the state and a general lack of freedom for the public to criticize state policies.

Professional Factors

The second dimension of the model represents professional factors such as individual journalistic values and the autonomy of individual journalists within media institutions. Media sociologists Windahl and Rosengren (1976, 1978) suggested that professionalization can be approached using two main perspectives: individual professionalization and collective professionalization. Individual professionalization is a form of socialization. The individual practitioner *qua* individual internalizes a positive view of education and training for the work, special requirements for entering the occupation, and the concept that the occupation has autonomy and self-regulation. Collective professionalization is a process involving the whole profession as such, and as a service ideal. Collective professionalization possesses attributes such as the existence of a professional association, training of members, a code of conduct or ethics, degree of autonomy, claim of monopoly over certain types of work, and the expression of a service ideal. Despite various socialization processes, the worldview of the individual journalists nourished under the two types of professionalism cannot be assumed to be congruent with the readers. In some cases, there even existed a considerable discrepancy between journalists' worldview and the media stance. The expression found in the media content is thus an interaction between these collective and individual journalistic values.

The specific professional individual values of interest here are subsumed under the dimension of conservatism-liberalism. Conservatism is operationalized as journalists being averse to rapid change, the avoidance of extremes, and the support of the societal status quo. In this sense, journalists may sacrifice their autonomy and their professional values in favor of the state policy, media stance, and the socialization process of their environment. Liberalism is operationalized as journalists supporting social change and reform, individualism, competition, and free speech (McQuail, 1994). Journalists who are said to be liberal adhere strongly to their own worldview, professional codes, and their own ethical and professional standards. Figure 1 illustrates the four categories created by the interaction of state system and individual journalistic values. As can be seen in this figure, national press systems can be classified as democratic-conservative, democratic-liberal, authoritarian-conservative, or authoritarian-liberal.

Democratic-conservative media systems are those in which the political system is democratic but the professional values of the majority of journalists are conservative—that is, the professional system(s) in which they operate emphasize support of societal status quo. Conversely, in a democratic-liberal system, dissent and free speech are values supported by both the political system and the individual journalists within that system. Authoritarian-conservative systems officially control press content and professional values within media organizations support such constraints. Authoritarian-liberal systems are those in which official policies suppress dissent, but individuals within media organizations support social reform and display such support in their practice of journalism.

A Test Case

A case study was used to examine the new model in the context of actual media coverage of a specific event. An important innovation was testing of the model using data from international coverage of an event rather than purely domestic

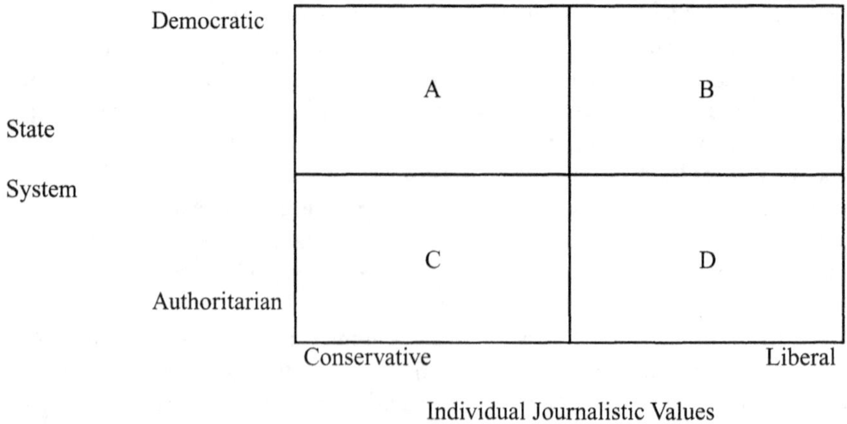

FIGURE 1 State system × Individual journalistic value model.

media coverage. Requirements for selection of the event were that it be covered by the media of several different countries (state system), tap into the journalistic values of individual journalists, and be of interest to the researchers. The event chosen was the 1996 debate between China and Japan over ownership of the Diaoyu or Senkaku Islands in the East China Sea. This debate provoked diplomatic rows and civil protests in Hong Kong, China, Japan, and Taiwan. These local protests tapped into issues of Chinese and Japanese nationalism and militarism—issues that might be expected to be linked to individual journalistic values. The sample consisted of newspaper coverage from Japan, Hong Kong, China, and the United States. U.S. media coverage was included because the main actors, Japan and China, saw the current problems as related to post–World War II U.S. Pacific foreign policy.

When previous models for the classification of national media systems are examined, little or no room is allowed for variation between countries that do not fall clearly into Western democratic or traditional Soviet Communist models. Table 1 identifies the categories under which each country studied here would be placed by each model and illustrates the problem of differentiating between these countries. Even when models based on economic factors are included such as those of Altschull (1984) and Akhavan-Majid and Wolf (1991) media in capitalist economies are grouped into the same category although clear differences exist. For example, the Four Theories model would place Hong Kong, Japan, and

TABLE 1
National Media Systems Classification

Country	Four Theories (1956)	Lowenstein (1971)	Hachten (1981)	Altschull (1984/1995)	Picard (1985)	Akhavan-Majid & Wolf (1991)
Hong Kong	Libertarian	1. Private/ multiparty/ govt. 2. Libertarian and social-authoritarian	Western	Market	Libertarian	Elite power group
Japan	Libertarian	1. Private 2. Libertarian	Western	Market	Libertarian	Elite power group
China	Soviet Communist	1. Government 2. Social-Authoritarian	Communist	Communitarian	Communist	
United States	Libertarian	1. Private 2. Social-libertarian	Western	Market	Western (social responsibility /libertarian)	Elite power group

the United States media in the same category, as would Hachten's (1981), Altschull's (1984/1995), and Akhavan-Majid and Wolf's (1991) models. Picard's (1985) model would group Hong Kong and Japanese media systems into the same category with U.S. media identified as Western (a combination of social responsibility and libertarian models).

Method

This study is based on a content analysis of Hong Kong, Japan, People's Republic of China, and U.S. media coverage of the issue in the period September 1 to September 30, 1996. Although selection of this period is somewhat arbitrary, the majority of events and media coverage occurred in the period between September 1 when Japanese coast guard ships prevented Taiwanese commercial boats from fishing in the area near the islands and September 26 when a journalist from Hong Kong drowned while part of a Hong Kong flotilla trying to reach the islands to protest the Japanese presence on them.

The sample. Media coverage in Hong Kong was extensive due to the emotional nature of the protests. The sample consisted of seven Hong Kong newspapers. A range of newspapers was chosen to account for both structural and individual dimensions of the model. These papers were the *South China Morning Post,* a prestigious English paper that was formerly extremely pro-British but now tends to adopt a more neutral tone; the *Oriental Daily,* a pro-China popular Chinese-language newspaper; the *Ming Pao,* representing the conservative intellectual press; two so-called China organs, the *Wen Wei Pao* and the *Ta Kung Pao;* the *Apple Daily,* a popular Chinese tabloid; and the *Hong Kong Economic Journal,* the most overtly critical paper in Hong Kong.

The Japanese sample consisted of two English-language daily newspapers, the *Asahi Evening News* and the *Japan Times.* Both are aimed at English-speaking communities in the country, and both carry material translated from local Japanese language media as well as material from international wire services.

At the present the Chinese sample consists only of the *China Daily.* However, this is an important source because it is the official English-language organ of the government of China. As such, articles and opinions carried in it are considered to express government opinions and policy as the government wishes them to be represented to the foreign community both inside and outside China. The U.S. sample consists of articles from the *New York Times, Wall Street Journal,* the *Minneapolis/St. Paul Star Tribune,* the Associated Press, and the Financial Times–Scripps Howard News Service.

Coding scheme. The coding scheme was developed to examine the general attitude of the article; article themes; what the article considered the issues concerned; who were considered the main actors; the level of action involved, that is, whether it was seen to be an international, government, individual, or political or social group action; and the solution suggested and agency, that is, who was seen to be eligible to take action in this situation. Papers were also coded for their political affiliation, if any, and the location of the article in the paper. Intercoder reliability for the Hong Kong sample was 87%.

For each coding category, conservatism or liberalism on the part of the journalist was defined and operationalized. In the first category—general attitude of the article—conservatism was categorized as support of the status quo, and liberalism as the opposite. The status quo is defined for each country as newspaper reports having an attitude favoring their own country and opposing another country; for example, Chinese newspapers supporting China's claims and opposing Japan's.

For the category of theme of the issue, conservatism was defined again as support of the status quo and emphasis on issues of sovereignty, historical claims, and moral obligation. Liberalism is defined as emphasis on modern, political, and social claims as well as indication of the issue as a matter for individuals, rather than governments.

In the category examining the level of action involved, conservatism is associated with perception of action being at the level of government whereas liberalism is associated with individual and social action. The same associations hold for the category of main actors, that is, who the main actors are seen to be. In examining agency, conservatism is again associated with support of the status quo; that is, each countries' newspapers perceiving their own country as having principal agency.

Results

Attitude and theme are important components of the model because they illuminate professional factors. By using a model that takes account of individual professionalism in addition to structural factors, a clearer picture can be built up of the actual operation of media systems. Using previous models discussed earlier in the article, Hong Kong and United States media are similar on the basis of structural factors. Whereas the structural dimensions of the countries examined are assumed and classified into various categories (such as authoritarian or democratic) according to the various models, the professional and individual dimensions are not articulated in these models. The data shed light on these individual and professional dimensions and their links with conservatism and liberalism.

Attitude. Conservatism as operationalized in the context of general attitudes in newspaper reports of the dispute over ownership of the Diaoyu/Senkaku Islands was defined as having an attitude supporting one's own country and opposing other countries. Looking at the data for support of one's own country and exhibition of negative attitudes toward other countries, China and Japan were the most conservative, with Hong Kong being somewhat less conservative, and the

United States as not at all conservative (Table 2). However, when the converse case was examined (anti-one's own country and pro-another country) distinctions become less clear-cut. News coverage in both the United States and China showed no negative attitudes toward one's own country nor attitudes in favor of another country. The U.S. results can be explained by 100% of its articles being neutral; that is, no stance was taken. An interesting result is that although the majority of results show Japanese media to be conservative, 9.75% of the articles contained anti-Japanese sentiments.

Theme. In the context of perceived theme of the issue, conservatism was linked to ideas of sovereignty, historical claim, and moral obligation. On this basis, Chinese and Japanese media again rank as more conservative than U.S. and Hong Kong media (Table 3). Liberalism was linked to ideas of modern and political claims, concepts of social obligation, and perception of the issue as being an

TABLE 2
Aggregated Content Analysis: General Attitude of Newspaper Coverage

	General Attitude	Hong Kong (1,378)	Japan (41)	China (16)	United States (12)
Conservatism	Pro-own country	5.40%	12.2%	81.13%	0%
	Anti-other country	12.49%	7.3%	46.88%	0%
Liberalism	Anti-own country	1.96%	9.75%	0%	0%
	Pro-other country	7.56%	0%	0%	0%
	Neutral	3.75%	80.5%	0%	100%

Note. For all tables percentage is average proportion (i.e., total percentage across categories divided by number of amalgamated categories).

TABLE 3
Aggregated Content Analysis: Perceived Theme of the Issue

	Theme of the Issue	Hong Kong (1,378)	Japan (41)	China (16)	United States (12)
Conservatism	Sovereignty Historical claim Moral obligation	29.4%	52.8%	64.58%	30.55%
Liberalism	Modern claim Political claim Social obligation	3.04%	6.09%	3.125%	8.33%
	Individual matter	(8.8%)	(0%)	(0%)	(8.33%)
	Other	0%	17%	0%	83.33%

individual matter. On this basis U.S. media are ranked as the most liberal followed by Japanese, Chinese, and Hong Kong media. However, if the single category of individual concern as the main theme is isolated from the other categories, Hong Kong and U.S. media rank as the most liberal (Table 3). This is important because individualism is a key definition of the notion of liberalism.

Main actors. Two further categories are considered together because they measure the individual values of the journalist using the same operationalization of conservatism and liberalism. These categories are those of perception of main actors in the issue and the level of action. Conservatism is linked with ideas about government being the main actor in social and political situations and liberalism is linked with ideas about social or political groups as well as individuals being important actors.

In the category of main actors, Chinese and Japanese media are the most conservative followed by members of the media in the U.S., then Hong Kong. However, on the liberalism scale, U.S. media are the most liberal followed by Japan, Hong Kong, and China (Table 4). In the category examining level of action, Japanese and Chinese media are the most conservative, followed by U.S. and Hong Kong media. However, if factors linked with liberalism are considered the same pattern occurs as in the category of actors; that is, U.S. media rank as the most liberal followed by Japanese, Hong Kong, then Chinese media (Table 4).

Agency. In the category of agency, conservatism is associated with maintenance of the status quo and the granting of agency to one's own country. Agency is defined here as which country is seen to be eligible to take action. Liberalism is associated with granting agency to actors other than one's own country. In this category, Chinese and Japanese media grant the most agency to their own country, whereas Hong Kong and U.S media grant the least (Table 5). Conversely, U.S. and

TABLE 4
Aggregated Content Analysis: Main Actors, Level of Action, and Agency

	Agency	Hong Kong (1,378)	Japan (41)	China (16)	United States (12)
Main actors	Government	52.6%	87.8%	100%	66.66%
	Social or political group	20.39%	47.58%	18.75%	58.3%
Level of action	Individuals Government	28.95%	56.05%	46.88%	29.15%
	Social or political group	10.78%	29.27%	6.25%	20.83%
	Individuals				

TABLE 5
Aggregated Country Comparisons: Agency

		Hong Kong (1,378)	Japan (41)	China (16)	United States (12)
Agency	Own country	3.02%	15.83%	25%	0%
	Other country	5.75%	1.06%	2.27%	17.24%
	Other	3.3%	0%	0%	16.66%

Hong Kong media grant the greatest amount of agency to other countries. Thus, U.S. and Hong Kong media are more liberal than Chinese and Japanese media.

Discussion

Based on these results, extremes of conservatism and liberalism on the part of journalists can be clearly identified. It is clear that the values of U.S. journalists as manifested in news coverage of debate over ownership of the Diaoyu/Senkaku Islands are liberal, whereas the values of Chinese journalists are conservative. Japanese media are clearly less conservative than Chinese media whereas they tend in the majority of categories to be much more conservative than U.S. media and somewhat more conservative than Hong Kong media.

Using the model incorporating journalistic values and state systems, and the data gathered from the case study, the media systems of China, Japan, Hong Kong, and the United States can be differentiated as shown in Figure 2. The data clearly differentiate

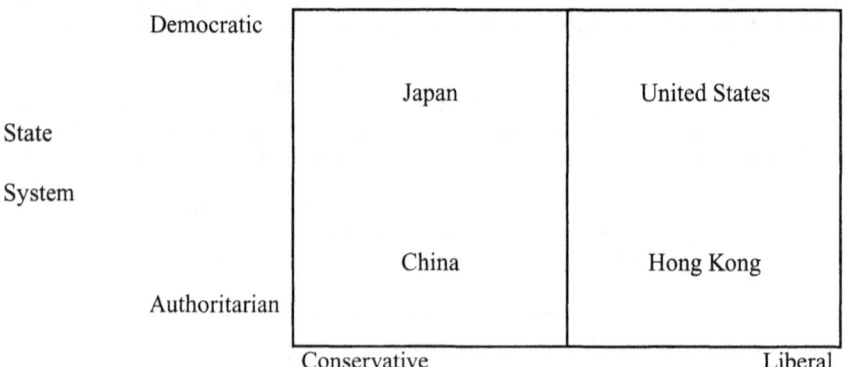

FIGURE 2 National classification under State system × Individual journalistic value model.

countries that share similar structural factors but in which individual journalists operate under different levels of professional autonomy. The Japanese system is seen to be democratic-conservative, contrasted with the U.S. democratic-liberal system. China's media system is authoritarian-conservative compared with Hong Kong's authoritarian-liberal system. This contrasts strongly with the way in which earlier models from the *Four Theories* onward tended to group Hong Kong, Japanese and U.S. media systems with China presented as a stark contrast or ignored entirely.

In addition to providing a greater level of differentiation between media systems, this model provides a link between structural factors and professional practice lacking in earlier normative models that reduced media coverage to a single structural dimension.

CONCLUSION

The study of comparative media systems and the development of philosophies of the press have long histories in the field of mass communication. Dominick (1994) argued that this is because of the implications for media freedom of relationships between the government and media. In any analysis of national systems, their media structures and institutions, as well as their relationship with political and economic structures, must be part of the picture because these relationships and structures are integral to the content, distribution, and reception of information in a society. Previous models describing or theorizing about national media systems have limited the power of their analysis by emphasizing a Cold War characterization of political systems. Models incorporating economic perspectives have increased the analytical power of these models but leave out those actors actually involved in the production of media. Incorporation of value systems of individual journalists as a level of categorization allows for differentiation between countries that would otherwise be categorized as similar on the basis of state or economic system.

This new model incorporates the dimensions of individual journalistic autonomy and the structures of state policy. It thus increases understanding of press systems and the societies in which these systems exist.

One main question remains: Can this approach be generalized across issues, media, and countries? Theories of national press systems have largely remained theories; that is, philosophical and normative proscriptions. By the use of content analysis of media coverage of an actual event, this new model has already moved beyond proscription to description and empirical analysis. Newspapers remain the medium of focus because they traditionally are closely tied to the political power structure and exhibit clearly the different institutional and structural constraints operating on the production of news. Although as a cross-national research and historical inquiry, newspapers also remain the most accessible resources for our studies, the proposed model allows for analysis of other specific media forms and structures insofar as the two levels of analysis are not medium dependent. That is, state systems operate at a political level above media systems, and journalistic values are incorporated in the individual journalist and not on the medium per se. Thus, this model is readily applicable in other media and country contexts where issues exist that cross these national boundaries.

Similarly the operationalization of conservatism and liberalism is based on individual journalistic values that go beyond coverage of specific issues. That is, the method employed here could be used with virtually any issue provided that a range of newspapers from each country (or other media) and a range of pieces from each newspaper (or other medium) are incorporated into the model to decrease the effect of variance due to individual journalistic differences and allow for analysis of national similarities and differences. For further studies, it would be essential to apply the method and model to different issues within a set of countries to see whether obtained differentiations hold across issues.

REFERENCES

Akhavan-Majid, R., & Wolf, G. (1991). American mass media and the myth of libertarianism: Toward an "elite power group" theory. *Critical Studies in Mass Communication, 8,* 139–151.

Altschull, H. (1995). *Agents of power: The media and public policy.* New York: Longman. (Original work published 1984)

Dominick, J. R. (1994). *The dynamics of mass communication.* New York: McGraw-Hill.

Hachten, W. (1981). *The world news prism.* Ames: Iowa State University.

Hall, S. (1982). The rediscovery of ideology. In J. Curran, M. Gurevitch, & J. Woollacott (Eds.), *Mass communication and society* (pp. 56–90). London: Edward Arnold.

McQuail, D. (1994). *Mass communication theory: An introduction.* London: Sage.

Merrill, J., & Lowenstein, R. (1979). *Media, messages and men: New perspectives in communication.* New York: Longman. (Original work published 1971)

Murdoch, G. (1982). Large corporations and the control of the communications industries. In M. Gurevitch, T. Bennett, J. Curran, & J. Woollacott (Eds.), *Culture, society and the media* (pp. 118–150). London: Methuen.

Picard, R. (1985). *The press and the decline of democracy: The democratic socialist response in public policy.* Westport, CT: Greenwood.

Siebert, F., Peterson, T., & Schramm, W. (1956). *Four theories of the press: The authoritarian, libertarian, social responsibility, and Soviet communist concepts of what the press should be and do.* Urbana: University of Illinois.

Williams, R. (1977). *Marxism and literature.* Oxford, England: Oxford University Press.

Windahl, S., & Rosengren, K. E. (1976). The professionalization of Sweden journalists. *Gazette, 22*(3), 140–149.

Windahl, S., & Rosengren, K. E. (1978). Newsmen's professionalization: Some methodological problems. *Public Opinion Quarterly, 55,* 466–473.

Wright, C. R. (1986). *Mass communication: A sociological perspective* (3rd ed.). New York: Random House.

National Identities, Structure, and Press Images of Nations: The Case of Japan and the United States

Catherine A. Luther
Department of Broadcasting
University of Tennessee

The main theoretical supposition of this study is that press disseminated images of nations are largely manifestations of national identities. It is assumed that even with structural changes in objective political economic conditions, coterminous changes in images may not take place. To examine this supposition, samples of press writings in the United States and Japan were qualitatively analyzed. U.S.–Japan relations from the mid-1970s to the mid-1990s were used as the study's context and time frame. The findings show that, although national identities appear to be playing a role in image formations, structural conditions also appear to be influencing the form of the images.

The study of images of nations has been a major area of research interest for many scholars in the discipline of international communication. In an effort to understand factors that may shape international relations, scholars have taken up the area of studying images of nations, especially those images disseminated by various press systems (e.g., Bookmiller & Bookmiller, 1992; Gerbner, 1991; Hashem, 1995; Hermann, 1985; Sreberny-Mohammadi, 1985). An underlying assumption that tends to exist in these studies is that the political economic structural conditions between nations are the prime molders of these images.[1] The assumption is that images are reflective of the international

---
[1] The classical notion of political economic structure is used here. It is understood as the social structure, processes, and relations that constitute the production, distribution, and consumption of resources. The major underlying assumption of this notion is that the actors are rational and goal-oriented beings (see Mosco, 1996).

Requests for reprints should be sent to Catherine A. Luther, Department of Broadcasting, College of Communication, University of Tennessee-Knoxville, 333 Communication Building, Knoxville, TN 37996. E-mail: cluther@utk.edu

political economic hierarchical order and as the order shifts, so too do the images.

Even if images of nations tend to be initially formed based on structural disparities among nations, however, one must question whether such images would necessarily change with changes in structure. If inequitable political economies were transformed toward more of a balance, would images of nations change in concert with such transformations? When considering the work by scholars such as Edward Said, one gets the sense that something more ingrained may be sustaining images of nations. In his examination of images of non-Western nations found in Western literature, Said saw the power structure as responsible for the creation of the images, but also emphasized that the images became accepted forms of consciousness by Westerners (Said, 1979, 1994). The images became representative of the Westerners' accepted sense of identity vis-à-vis other nations and people.

Taking this notion that images may represent national identities, the contention of this study is that press disseminated images of nations are not necessarily determined by political economic structural conditions, but are largely manifestations of a nation's sense of identity in relation to other nations. Thus, even with structural shifts in objective political economic conditions, coterminous changes in images may not take place.

To examine whether images of nations tend to be illustrative of an overarching national psyche and to see whether image formations are influenced by shifts in structural conditions, samples of press writings in the United States and Japan were qualitatively analyzed. U.S.–Japan relations from 1975 to 1995 were used as the study's context and time frame. Images of the United States and of Japan were classified as representations each nation had of itself and the other nation. The main theoretical suppositions were that consistency in images of nations could be found in press content, that those images of nations would reflect national identities, and that the images would tend to be consistent across time in spite of political economic changes.

NATIONAL IDENTITY AND PRESS IMAGES

Anderson (1991) wrote of national identity in ethereal terms. Unlike certain scholars who suggested national identities emanate from structures within a demarcated territory and who connected the concept of identity with territoriality (e.g., Gellner, 1983; Rokkan & Urwin, 1983), Anderson acknowledged that territorial boundaries may indeed exist, but, for the people who live within those perimeters, they are essentially imagined boundaries. As Anderson (1991) wrote:

It is *imagined* because the members of even the smallest nation will never know most of their fellow-members, meet them, or even hear of them, yet in the minds of each lives the image of their communion. . . . It is imagined as a *community*, because, regardless of the actual inequality and exploitation that may prevail in each, the nation is always conceived as a deep, horizontal comradeship. (pp. 6–7)

Anderson asserted that the advent of printed language played a crucial role in the building of "imagined" communities—national identities. The expressions of language were able to bring together individuals from diverse backgrounds into a single overarching collectivity.

If printed language played such an important role in the past, it is perhaps safe to assume that in present-day societies, the press, or more broadly the media, may be continuing to play an important role in reflecting and promoting national identities among various nation-states. In fact, some scholars have asserted that governing elites often intentionally use the press to build identification with the state. For example, Schudson (1994) wrote that "the modern nation-state self-consciously uses language policy, formal education, collective rituals, and mass media to integrate citizens and ensure their loyalty" (p. 22). According to this view, the power elites deliberately manipulate the press or other forms of media to create social integration and a common identity to maintain stability within the nation. Whether such manipulation is overt depends on whether the society is totalitarian or democratic.

Even without overt or indirect external pressures by the elite powers, however, when it comes to international issues or events, the members of the press have shown signs of having a natural inclination to support a particular collective identity. This natural inclination to support one's own collective identity appears to be especially true in nations with long histories of established mass media. For example, in an analysis of various forms of literature, Spurr (1994) presented journalists and writers, from nations with long media histories, as expressing, in their writings, whole-hearted commitments to their own collective backgrounds. The commitment to a national collective in these writings appears to have been natural expressions, on the part of the authors, of their own sense of national identities.

In line with Spurr's (1994) work, in this research, an attempt was made to see whether such manifestations of national identities could be unfolded by analyzing U.S.–Japan press images within the context of U.S.–Japan relations. National identity was defined as a specific form of social identity embodying shared core values and norms associated with the nation-state, enclosing a nation's sense of emotive salience vis-à-vis other nations. The research also went a step further in attempting to see if the images tended to change in concert with political economic structural changes between the United States and Japan.

METHOD

To ascertain the type of images conveyed in news items from the United States and Japan, a qualitative analysis of news articles and editorials concerning U.S.–Japan relations in the U.S.'s *New York Times* and Japan's *Yomiuri* were conducted.[2] Based on the finding from other research that content and perspectives regarding international issues tend not to significantly vary between elite mainstream newspapers (e.g., De Lange, 1998; Nokes, 1990; Suzuki, 1993), both here in the United States and in Japan, it was surmised that content in these two papers would at least suggest the type of images that would be conveyed by other mainstream press within the context of U.S.–Japan relations. The *New York Times* is published in the city of New York and is often referred to as the U.S. newspaper of record; the *Yomiuri* is a national paper. Some may raise a concern regarding the comparability of these two newspapers. However, as many researchers have pointed out, the *New York Times* comes closer than any other to a national newspaper in the United States, being read across the country and frequently setting an agenda or providing articles for other city newspapers (Chang, 1993; Gitlin, 1980; Merrill, 1968). The *Yomiuri* has enjoyed the largest circulation of any Japanese newspaper since the mid-1970s and is said to represent Japan's mainstream ideas in Japan (Haruhara & Amenomori, 1994; Yomiuri Newspaper, 1996).

A systematic sample of news articles and editorials was randomly drawn from indexes of the *New York Times* and the *Yomiuri* for every other month of every fourth year, of the time frame 1975 to 1995. Only those items listed in the indexes under the subheadings of (a) U.S.–Japan general relations, (b) U.S.–Japan security issues, and (c) U.S.–Japan economic issues were randomly drawn based on an established sampling rule.[3] The sampling rule yielded 259 news items from the U.S. newspaper and 345 news items from the Japanese newspaper.

Major themes and discursive patterns consistently presented across time in the two newspapers' sampled texts were noted to identify images. More specifically, based on methods used in discourse analysis studies (e.g., de Beaugrande, 1985; Fairclough, 1992; van Dijk, 1988), in analyzing the news items, an effort was made to ascertain the following: (a) use of metaphors, (b) use of historical

---

[2]Note that the editions of the *Yomiuri* used in this study are not the international editions, but rather the domestic editions.

[3]Sampling rule was as follows: If the total number of items listed under one subheading was under 40, every item was sampled and examined; if the total number of items listed under one subheading was between 41 and 100, every other item was sampled and examined; if the total number of items listed under one subheading was between 101 and 200, every fifth item was sampled and examined; if the total number of items listed under one subheading was between 201 and 300, every seventh item was sampled and examined; if the total number of items listed under one subheading was 301 or more, every ninth item was sampled and examined.

analogies, (c) key words (e.g., the use of adjectives/pronouns for the country in question), and (d) miscellaneous key phrases that express a certain image of the country in question.

To determine whether national identity might be underpinning the images, each item was examined for consistent themes that echoed the social values and norms of the nation in question. To gain an understanding of the major values and norms of each nation, research pertaining to values and norms of the United States and of Japan (e.g., Lipset, 1990; Reischauer, 1995) was reviewed before initiating the study. This provided a better ability to judge the existence of references to values and norms within the news items. In addition, items were examined for recurring characterizations of a nation (often through the use of metaphors and analogies) in terms of dispositional qualities in relation to that nation. Dispositional qualities refer to any distinguishing mental character or temperament; they are internal and psychologically based (Fiske & Taylor, 1991).

For each item, the themes, the components of the themes, and any tension (contradiction) between the themes were noted on a 3 × 5 index card. What was found was that although certain contradictory themes were presented in some of the news items, when reading the entire item, one central theme—a macroproposition—always came to light. The notes made on each index card were then systematically reviewed to ascertain the central themes. Those themes or macropositions, if they were consistently repeated across the time frame, were then used to identify the major images.[4]

After analysis of the U.S. and Japanese news items, additional primary and secondary sources were analyzed. A sample of news items from two U.S. weekly news magazines, *Time* and *Newsweek*, was analyzed. Every item under the subheading of U.S. and Japan foreign relations in the *Guide to Periodical Literature* was chosen for analysis for each year of the time frame. The procedure yielded a sample size of 40 news items.

In terms of additional Japanese primary sources, only the Japanese-language editions of *Time* and *Newsweek* are available, and no Japanese counterparts to such weekly news magazines exist. Thus, secondary sources related to the images in Japan of Japan and of the United States were studied to see whether they supported the images derived from the *Yomiuri*.

To examine whether images tended to remain consistent or shift across the time frame in conjunction with changes in structural conditions, careful note was taken

---

[4]Note that two other individuals, one Japanese and one American, also reviewed roughly 10% of the sampled news items for interpretation using the same method used by the primary researcher. The individuals were asked to note the major themes they believed were being conveyed in the items with regard to Japan and the United States. An agreement rate of more than 90% was reached with both researchers. Silverman (1993) was used as a guide for carrying this out.

with regard to when the images tended to emerge and wane in the news items. Along with this, a review of research (e.g., Buckley, 1992; LaFeber, 1997) regarding U.S.–Japan relations was conducted to allow for an understanding of the structural conditions, and any major fluctuations in these conditions, between the two nations during the time frame.

U.S.–JAPAN RELATIONS FROM 1975 TO 1995: MAJOR CONTEXTUAL ISSUES

Even with Japan's resumption of national sovereignty in 1951, following the U.S. occupation of Japan, Japan had continued to rely on the United States economically, politically, and militarily. The mid-1970s, however, represented a turning point for Japan. By the mid-1970s, Japan emerged as the third largest economic power in the world, albeit still behind the United States. Foreign direct investments had previously been limited to the development and production of industrial raw materials; but now, Japan began a surge of direct Japanese capital investments in areas that would allow a boost in Japanese production capabilities and would circumvent some of the growing protectionist policies abroad (Fukui, 1992; Reischauer, 1995). Juxtaposed to Japan's striking economic growth rate was the steady decay of the United States's relative economic and political weight in the international community. Coming out of the Vietnam fiasco and having to face its growing rate of inflation, the United States had to come to terms with its decline as the foremost international powerhouse (Walter, 1987). The asymmetrical relationship between the United States and Japan that had been maintained in the first few postwar decades was beginning to reach a certain degree of symmetry.

By the 1980s, a reversal of fortunes for Japan and the United States became apparent. An increase in its foreign exports led Japan toward a trade surplus with the United States that ran as high as $60 billion in the mid-1980s (Reischauer, 1995). With the growing United States trade deficit with Japan as the backdrop, market shares and the opening up of markets became issues of prominence. The opening of Japan's beef, citrus, and rice markets to United States imports were notable issues. In addition, Japan's large shares in the automobile, machine tool, and semiconductor markets in the United States were also in the forefront.

The 1990s did witness a weakening of Japan's economic power. With the collapse of its financial institutions and its loss of prime overseas investments, Japan suffered a serious recession beginning in the early 1990s. Yet, even with such economic concessions and difficulties, Japan still recorded annual trade surpluses with the United States. In the military realm, as the United States continued to cut back on overseas military operations, Japan began to increase self-defense powers. The 1990s saw Japan's first engagement in world peacekeeping operations using its self-defense forces.

Within such a context, the reporting of U.S.–Japan issues by the *New York Times* and the *Yomiuri* from 1975 to 1995 did reveal consistent images each nation had of itself and of the other nation. Major thematic images were found in the news items examined in this research, and national identities appeared to be manifested in these images. The surrounding structural conditions, however, also appeared to impinge on the image formations.

IMAGES FROM THE *NEW YORK TIMES*

The United States: "Defender of the Free World" Still Standing Strong

Within the context of U.S.–Japan relations, throughout the mid-1970s to the mid-1990s, objective references to the decline in the United States's economic stature appear in the U.S. news items. The growing deficit, the decline in U.S. exports, high unemployment rates, and problems associated with U.S. production capabilities are examples of the characteristics appearing in a number of the items (e.g., Ferguson, 1987, p. A25; Grove, 1987, p. C3; "Shape Up Japan," 1983, p. A19). Alongside these negative descriptions, however, the rhetoric of the United States as still being inherently strong or as having the ability to recapture its strength comes to the fore.

The idea that was underscored in the news items is that even with the United States's various political and economic problems, it was still in a position of strength, or had the means to regain the strength, and was still the torch-bearer for democracy. For example, in an article appearing in September 1975, mention was made of the "'U.S. responsibilities that flow from our world leadership position'" (Halloran, 1975, p. A10). Even as the deterioration of the United States's power began to become evident, the newspaper items referred to the United States in such terms as the "defender of the free world," "a greater power," and the "financial center of the world" (e.g., Faux, 1987, p. A1; Clines, 1983, p. A4; Gwetzman, 1983, p. B2).

Although acknowledging Japan's rise in its economic capabilities, the strength of the United States and Japan's dependency on the United States were emphasized. For example, a passage from a 1987 editorial read: "Japan needs the American market and it also needs American security protection. Japan also needs America as the necessary stabilizer of an orderly world system with economies truly open to international trade" ("How About," 1987, p. A31). This idea that Japan was an insecure nation that needed the continued guidance of the United States was frequently conveyed in the U.S. newspaper items. Moreover, this insecurity was often not attributed to conditional terms, but rather, more psychological terms. Japan was painted as being inherently fragile.

Japan as Inherently Weak and Ineffective

The idea that Japan was an inherently weak nation that needed the continued guidance of the United States was a notion that was frequently conveyed in the U.S. newspaper items. For example, after describing the economic gains Japan had been able to achieve, a *New York Times* journalist concluded by proposing the thought that, despite their gains, the Japanese were not able to come to terms with their new international standing. The journalist wrote, "They [Japanese] don't think of themselves as number one in the world, despite their successes; they are full of self-doubt and wonder how long their success will last. They know that their security . . . depends . . . in the end, on the military and economic policies of the United States" (Reston, 1979, p. D21).

In another article, segments of a speech made by the U.S. Ambassador to Japan, James D. Hodgson, to an audience in Japan were accentuated. In the segments highlighted, while congratulating Japan for its continued economic expansion, Hodgson went on to state that despite such growth, the United States needed "'to remain aware of several special considerations that mark both Japan's internal circumstances and its role in the world.'" The ambassador continued to remark,

> I have in mind such things as the vulnerability of your economy to external forces, your limited indigenous natural resources, your focal Northeast Asia location near 'superpower' territory, your acute allergy to external surprise, your extensive Asian interests and your rather residual sense of insecurity. (Halloran, 1975, p. A10)

This notion of Japan's insecurity was also translated as being a primary reason for what the United States saw as Japan's continued ineptness in the political realm.

What was conveyed in the *New York Times* news items was the perception in the United States that Japan was lacking the propensity to be a world political leader. One journalist described Japan as enveloped by "a vague sense of aimless drift in politics, the economy and diplomacy" ("Tokyo Is Caught," 1975, p. A5). In a similar vein, in another article, the journalist wrote that "the Japanese have no coherent, identifiable foreign policy" and that "Japan seems to be drifting aimlessly." The journalist went on to assert that the reasons for this "are found more within Japan itself," in its "consensus" society and its lingering "mentality of a 'shima-guni,' the island nation" ("Japan Drifts," 1975, p. D3).[5]

Several news items, in describing Japan's anemic political capabilities, stressed the idea that Japan was still very much dependent on the United States for political guidance. For example, one article referred to Japan's "diplomatic inertia," and

---

[5]Note that the phrase "shima-guni" has connotations of Japan being an insular country, wanting to keep out foreigners. The phrase originated during Japan's Tokugawa era when the nation was effectively closed to the outside world (Hall, 1982).

described how Japan continued "to rely on the United States diplomatically and militarily" ("Japanese Fearful," 1975, p. A17). Taking a more critical tone, a journalist wrote in an article from the 1990s, "Japan is a global power, but incapable of initiative, in a sense immature, avoiding asking itself what it should do but asking what others, perhaps unfairly, expect of it" (Lewis, 1991, p. D25).

Some may argue that the writings in the U.S. newspapers may be interpreted as reflecting the actual political culture in Japan, that the prose in these writings simply painted a fairly accurate picture of Japan's leadership capabilities, stemming from certain underlying sociopsychological characteristics of the Japanese. Scholars (e.g., Martin & Stronach, 1992) who have studied Japan's political culture have pointed out, for example, that the political culture is one that is based on harmony, rather than conflict, and that it is based on pragmatism, rather than ideology, where choices are often made without logical consistencies. And yet, the writings in the U.S. newspapers appeared to go beyond attempting to accurately portray a system based on a certain political culture; more emotive responses to Japan that appear to be based on a sense of identity are reflected. A tendency to distrust the Japanese and a reluctance to acknowledge Japan as a notable international player are present.

Even in terms of discussing the economic accomplishments of Japan, the newspaper items evinced a tendency to disparage the means by which those successes were attained or to take some form of credit for the successes. The voices signified in the items were those that disparaged the accomplishments of Japan. Some of the articles expressed the view that Japan was only able to make economic strides due to the security provided by the United States, that Japan achieved economic success due to the "free ride" it enjoyed in military matters (e.g., Haberman, 1983b, p. A3; Lohr, 1983, p. D1). More frequently, a deep-seated distrust of Japan and an accusatory tone of how Japan's gains were met are expressed.

Japan as Duplicitous and Unscrupulous

One of the thematic images of Japan that was conveyed by the newspaper items was that of a nation that managed to acquire economic achievements through unprincipled and dishonest means. The news items referred to the "unfair" competition, "price rigging," and the "self-serving policies" of Japan as having led to Japan's economic achievements ("A Very," 1983, p. A1; "Chip Makers," 1987, p. A21; Pollack, 1987, p. D1). Within the context of trade negotiations, the Japanese were described as only paying "lip service," as not playing "fair," as not living "up to its promises," and as engaging in "duplicity and foot-dragging" (Haberman, 1987, p. A14; "A Trade," 1987, p. D3; Kilborn, 1987a, p. D1).

Much space was devoted in a number of the articles and editorials to the "Japanese Establishment" or the so-called Japan, Inc. that was said to run the country (e.g., Dahlby, 1979, p. A9; Farnsworth, 1987, p. A37; Scott-Stokes, 1979, p. A3).

Far from simply explaining Japan, Inc. and perhaps the underlying cultural reasons for the system's existence, however, many of the news items conveyed a perception in the United States that such a system existed in Japan due to the less than virtuous character of the nation or people. The Japanese were characterized, for example, as "untrustworthy," as "neurotic," as "corporate gangsters" using "treacherous economic karate," and even as "Asian devils" ("Japanese Competition," 1983, p. C3; Haberman, 1983a, p. A1; Kristoff, 1995, p. A12; "The Dollar's," 1987, p. A30). Such pejorative descriptions of Japan or its people appeared to increase in intensity during the late 1980s and into the 1990s. In particular, the U.S. newspaper items' use of wartime metaphors and analogies was heightened.

Themes of War

It is during this later part of the time frame that phrases such as "trade war," "crossed swords," "bloody battle," "economic security," "weapons," "arms control talks of the new age," "retaliation," "unarmed," and "heavily armed" become quite apparent in the articles and editorials (e.g., Christopher, 1987, p. A31; Farnsworth, 1991, p. D1; Greenhouse, 1995, p. D1; Sanger & Weiner, 1995, p. A1; "When Spies," 1995, p. D4). For example, covering the United States's accusations that Japan was not adequately opening up its markets to the United States, one article quoted Secretary of State James Baker as stating, "'Nobody wants a trade war, but nobody wants to be a patsy either'" (Boyd, 1987, p. D7). In a similar mode, Agricultural Secretary Richard Lying was quoted in another article as saying,

> "They are not going to start a trade war with us, with the amount of dollar trade they have with the United States. . . . But we may start a trade war with them accidentally. It's because they make the country so angry. If they make Americans angry enough it will cost them dearly." (Kilborn, 1987b, p. D5)

More direct analogies related to World War II also appeared in the news items. For example, in one article, the journalist wrote, "the Japanese have achieved with yen what their fathers could not with bombs" (Reinhold, 1991, p. A1). In another article, the words of White House Chief of Staff Howard Baker were paraphrased. Baker was said to have stated that "'Japan has not given up its wartime goal of conquest but now pursues it by economic instead of military means'" ("Enough," 1987, p. A31). The same article also quoted Representative Jack Brooks of Texas as saying, "'God Bless Harry Truman. He dropped two of them. He should have dropped four.'" In yet another article, the journalist wrote of how the Clinton administration was unified in its threat to "use its big stick" and its "willingness to use the blunt and ugly weapon of punitive sanctions to achieve its goal"; the journalist went on to quote Vice President Al Gore as saying, "'We're not going to blink'" (Sanger, 1995b, p. D5).

Although the World War II analogies tended to be extreme and tended to be conveyed through the quoting of individuals, in many of the news items that appeared during and after the late 1980s, images of war were relayed directly by the words conjured by the writers themselves. For example, in one article, the following observation was made: "Now that Japan is a major threat—and some of its greatest weapons are perceived to be cultural traditions like 'buying Japanese,' a conspiracy against foreigners and saving money fanatically—Japanese culture has been transformed into a threat" (Makin, 1987, p. C27). In a piece on trade friction between Japan and the United States, the journalist equated hostile threats made in the economic sphere in the late 1980s to the nuclear threat made during the height of the Cold War. The journalist wrote: "The economic situation today has a certain similarity to the threat of nuclear war in the 'postwar' world" (Silk, 1987, p. D2). In a similar vein, another journalist wrote, "Car parts never quickened Henry Kissinger's pulse. But one doesn't have to be in Geneva long to discover that divisions between America and Japan are the arms-control negotiations of the '90s" (Sanger, 1995a, p. A2).

Such wartime rhetoric also appeared to gain prominence in the late 1980s in the additional news sources examined, *Time* and *Newsweek*. Furthermore, the themes of U.S. strength, Japan's dependency, and Japan's ineffectiveness and duplicitous character found throughout the time frame in the *New York Times* also similarly appeared in these sources.

Major Themes in *Time* and *Newsweek*

U.S. fortitude and Japan's dependence on the United States were noticeably emphasized throughout this time frame in the examined *Time* and *Newsweek* news items. For example, in a 1975 *Newsweek* article, the journalists stressed that Japan still needed the United States's leadership guidance and was falling back to a "healthy" acknowledgment of its "heavy reliance on the Western giant [America]" (Deming, Kirsher, & van Voorst, 1975, p. 42). They then went on to report on Japan's failure to make a deal with the Arab nations regarding Japan's import of petroleum, without the "U.S. lead." The journalists quoted former U.S. ambassador to Japan Edwin Reischauer as stating that because of this failure "the Japanese realized that America was 'a much bigger and more important factor in their well-being'" (p. 44).

In a 1989 *Newsweek* article, the journalist discussed the economic and political achievements Japan had been able to make, but commented that Japan, with its propensity for not being able to take on leadership roles, would never be able to "be a power that bestrode the world in the postwar years, or even one resembling Washington . . . today" (Martz, 1989, p. 15). The author went on to state how "the United States will remain Tokyo's biggest market and a growing outlet for investment" and how Japan would "rely on Washington's extended power to maintain world peace" (p. 16).

While acknowledging the vast economic gains that Japan had been able to garner and the increasing role it was beginning to play in the military realm, in the examined *Newsweek* and *Time* articles, like in the *New York Times* news items, Japan was still portrayed as being inept, unsure, and lacking the ability to be a true international leader. For example, in a 1975 *Newsweek* article, the journalist conveyed the point that Japan did not have what it took to become a real political power, and emphasized that Japan managed to get along in the international arena simply because of Japan's "national character marked by vast adaptability . . . and a knack for solving the most difficult problems through consensus and accommodation" (Deming, 1975, p. 53). The journalist ended his story by stating, "the Japanese have turned muddling through into another Oriental art" (p. 53).

In another *Newsweek* article, the journalist conceded to Japan's rise economically and militarily by stating facts and figures, but throughout the article emphasized the theme that Japan was not equipped to handle such power. For example, the journalist wrote:

> "Can Japan become a world leader? The answer to that is probably no," says Donald C. Hellmansn, an Asia expert at the University of Washington. "Any world leader must be able to articulate a set of ideals and values. You've got to have a legitimacy beyond power." (Martz, 1989, p. 15)

Using an old Japanese proverb that states that "the nail that sticks out, gets hammered down," the journalist later wrote, "The Japanese change slowly and hesitate to take leadership in anything: to be out front on an issue is to be a nail sticking out" (p. 20).

Also alluding to the disposition of Japan as preventing the nation from being a leader, in another *Newsweek* article the journalist described Japan as being in an "uncoordinated emotional confusion" brought about by the "dizzying speed of Japan's advance, and the sense of being caught precariously between a safer, consensus-oriented past and the more fluid demands of the future" (Platt, 1989, p. 18).

In a *Time* article, the journalist chose a title, "From Superrich to Superpower," that would relay the idea of Japan as being strong; yet, the actual focus of the entire article was on how Japan could not handle the wealth that it had accumulated and on how it could never be a power like the United States, due to Japan's innate characteristics. The journalist described the Japanese as being "still torn by conflicting emotions over their proper place in the sun," and stated that "the Japanese are sometimes seen by outsiders as lacking clear goals for their country or any abiding sense of how to put their wealth and power to use" (Greenwald, 1988, p. 29).

Even as Japan began to show tangible signs of trying to assert itself on the international world stage in the 1990s, by such demonstrations as demanding International Monetary Fund and World Bank voting rights and by expressing a desire to be placed on the U.N. Security Council, the articles tended to place doubts on

Japan's actual ability to carry out a more internationally oriented leadership role. For example, in a 1991 *Time* article, the journalist stressed that the "'Japanese are not willing to make the hard political choices,'" stating that Japan's "foreign policy lacks focus or clear direction" and is "never bold" (Hillenbrand, 1991, p. 42). Thus, the image that is relayed by these articles is that Japan is essentially unequipped, for psychologically related reasons, to be a significant international player and power.

It is interesting that the articles, although acknowledging the objective economic strengths of Japan, not only stressed how Japan was not psychologically equipped to handle such strengths, but also tended to emphasize the negative features of Japan's society in general. For example, a journalist writing in *Newsweek* commented:

> It is possible for Americans to admire the Japanese; it is possible to fear them. But there is no reason to envy them. For all their country's economic power, most Japanese live in straitened circumstances, with a relatively low standard of living, long working hours, cramped housing and scant opportunity for recreation. They endure a political system that does not respond to ordinary citizens, an educational system that puts brutal pressure on the young and a family culture that belittles women, by Western standards. (Christopher, 1989, p. 47)

In another *Newsweek* article, the journalist, although pointing out the wealth that Japan had accumulated, emphasized the social caveats of Japan. He wrote, for example, "Prices from everything from land to lunch boxes are absurdly high. Yet few complain, in part, because that would violate the taboo that has only been reinforced by the collective commitment to overcoming the devastation of World War II" (Powell, 1989, p. 45). In a sense, the articles appeared to be attempting to find drawbacks to Japan's success.

Also similar to the *New York Times* news items, characterizations of Japan as being unscrupulous appeared in the additional examined sources as well. For example, in a *Newsweek* article, a reference was made to a Central Intelligence Agency–funded report that portrayed Japan as a nation not to be trusted. In describing the report, the journalist wrote:

> According to a recent contract report written for the Central Intelligence Agency, they [Japanese] are "racist" and "amoral." Their international vision does not extend beyond an insatiable thirst for economic power, the report finds; what's more, they seek to "supplant" Western values and impose their own on the world. (Powell, 1991, p. 33)

As another example, in a *Time* article the journalist wrote,

> A broad range of Americans, knowledgeable and temperate ones at that, see Japan as insensitive and arrogant. . . . In some views Japan is already achieving economically what it failed to win by force of arms: a Greater East Asia Co-Prosperity Sphere. (Hillenbrand & Walsh, 1991, p. 70)

Taking a similar tone, in another *Newsweek* article, the journalist wrote of how Americans "see Japan's business-suited legions conquering worldwide markets, wiping out entire U.S. industries and planting their flag on blue-chip properties all over America" (Watson, 1991, p. 46).

In addition to portraying Japan as being unethical and duplicitous in national character, the additional examined articles, similar to the *New York Times* news items, also intensified their use of wartime rhetoric toward the end of this time frame. For example, in discussing U.S. demands for Japan to further open up its various trade markets to the United States, the journalist wrote in *Time* of how, despite the demands, Japan was "holding off the assault" (Desmond, 1994, p. 46). Other *Time* and *Newsweek* articles, as well, not only used the term *war* to describe the relationship between Japan and the United States in the late 1980s and early 1990s, but also used such war-related words as "retaliation," "threat," and "standoff" (e.g., Church, 1993, pp. 26–27; Lacayo, 1994, p. 41; Powell, 1993, p. 40). As is presented in the next section, such wartime rhetoric also appeared in the examined Japanese news items.

IMAGES FROM THE *YOMIURI*

During the early half of this time frame, from the mid-1970s to the mid-1980s, the prime image conveyed in the *Yomiuri* news items was that of Japan's uncertainty in terms of how to deal with the United States, and more generally, with the rest of the world powers. With regard to Japan's relationship with the United States, although signs of opposition were relayed in the items, they were balanced by suggestions of accepted deference toward the United States. By the late 1980s, however, clear expressions of a newly found confidence and a willingness to oppose the United States were conveyed by the news items. Moreover, the intensity of such confidence and open opposition came to the fore in the 1990s.

Japan: From *Happobijin* to Vocal Adversary

From the mid-1970s and into the 1980s, many of the news items conveyed a sense of Japan as struggling to break away from its psychological as well as material bonds with the United States (e.g., "Bei," 1979; "Kagou," 1975; "Taibei," 1975). A need to become more assertive toward the United States and not so vulnerable to U.S. needs, as well as to the needs of the outside world in general, were clearly manifested in the items. One editorial writer called for Japan's end to being a *happobijin*, one who tries to please everyone in every way, stating that this tendency on the part of Japan "only brings about a distrust" among the other countries ("Sanjuku," 1975, p. 1). Another editorial writer also alluded to the idea that Japan was out to please all, stating that Japan needed to become more adept at negotiating, and not rely on money to do its diplomatic talking ("Yomiuri," 1975a). In yet another editorial, the writer asserted that if Japan continued its *happobijin* posture in an effort to please and resolve friction between it and other countries, such a posture would soon catch up to Japan and become the key to further problems ("Sekai," 1983, p. 1).

Several editorials also expressed the idea that Japan was no longer as engrossed in the ways of the United States and that it needed to, and was attempting to, shed its propensity for simply following the lead of the United States in foreign policy making (e.g., "Chakuzitsu," 1979; "Nichibei Koushou," 1979). For example, in one editorial, a quote from former Prime Minister Suzuki was presented at the beginning of the editorial and was used as a central theme throughout the piece. The quote read, "Isn't it the case that if we continue to say 'yes, we'll do this and yes, we'll do that,' then no matter how much we do, the United States will not be satisfied in the least bit?" ("Shitsubo," 1983, p. 1). In another editorial, Prime Minister Yasuhiro Nakasone was applauded for having directly refused the United States's request to have Japan open its markets to U.S. oranges and beef ("Yomiuri," 1983).

Yet, during this earlier part of the time frame, despite such manifestations of opposition and the desire to break away, the news items also indicated Japan's unshakable tendency to fall back on relying on the United States for guidance and an inclination to acquiesce to U.S. demands ("Anpou," 1975; "Boeki," 1983; "Shijou," 1979; "Yomiuri," 1975b). For example, an article described how Japanese officials, despite lacking a supportive consensus on the issue, were scrambling to meet the "United States' strong demands" that Japan share its military technology with the United States, so that the plan could be in place when President Reagan arrived in Japan for his visit ("Buki," 1983, p. 2). Many of the news items suggested that Japan's tendency toward complying with the United States stemmed from its weakness toward authority and its concern for possible U.S. retaliation (e.g., "Nichibei Keizai," 1979; "Nichibei," 1983; "Yomiuri," 1979a; "Yomiuri," 1979b).

Whereas the newspaper items appearing from the mid-1970s and into the 1980s expressed an image of Japan as remaining submissive to the United States, despite its growing sense of confidence and its desire to break away from the United States, the news items appearing in the late 1980s and in the 1990s revealed a Japan that was becoming more comfortable in its world position and less willing to comply with the demands of the United States.

As what appeared to be manifestations of Japan's determined confidence, the words chosen by the journalists in reference to opposition against U.S. decisions and actions were more confrontational in nature during this later period. For example, in an editorial entitled, "Shape Up America," the writer discussed the need for the United States to get its own house in order and regain its lost qualities of leadership ("Amerika," 1987, p. 3). In another editorial, the writer asserted, "The Japanese people, who could not very well, up until this point, outwardly express dissatisfaction and discontent toward the United States, are gradually doing so now" ("Masatsu,"

1987, p. 3). In one article entitled "Toward the Bonds of Cooperation and Equality," the journalist stated that Japan had reached the point where it needed to cooperate with the United States on its own terms. The journalist quoted a Japanese scholar as stating, "Up until now, Japan really did not have a strategy of its own separate from the United States. Japan must now, while cooperating, prevent itself from further being at the United States' beck and call" ("Taitou," 1991, p. 1).

By the end of this chosen time frame, the news items reflected a Japan that was less apprehensive about speaking out against the United States and less willing to give in to U.S. demands so easily. In fact, in many of the items, Japan exhibited a newly found courage to renounce the actions and decisions of the United States, and to return U.S. threats of retaliation with threats of its own (e.g., "Bei-Shouheki," 1995; "Buhin," 1995; "Jishu," 1995; "Kijuku," 1995; "Kuruma," 1995). In an article pertaining to the negotiations that were taking place between Japan and the United States, regarding auto imports, the journalist quoted a leading Japanese official as stating that Japan was "fiercely fighting in a friendly manner" ("Bei Suuchi," 1995, p. 6). In another article, the journalist conveyed the thought that the United States could no longer assume that Japan would readily give in to its demands ("Keizai Chouhousen," 1995). While conveying such strength, the articles and editorials also exhibited a sense of pride in Japan.[6] This occurred even as Japan began to seriously experience its own economic woes in the 1990s. For example, in one editorial, the writer lauded the economic accomplishments of Japan and stressed that, despite Japan's recent economic difficulties, the country was in a "position of international importance" and that it needed to take up the responsibilities that came with such a position, that it needed to "lead in the establishment of a constructive theory for the new world economic system" ("Kijikutsuka," 1995, p. 3).

It is interesting to note that together with such displays of Japan's confidence in confronting the United States, in cases where Japan ultimately carried out the

---

[6]It is interesting to note that scholars examining popular culture in Japan have also reported this same sense of strength and pride in Japan as beginning to strikingly emerge in and after the mid-1980s in various forms of popular culture (i.e., books, films, etc.). These scholars have observed that a large number of books, in particular, began to emerge in Japan that articulated and celebrated Japan's unique values and traditions. Not only were these books published, but they also sold well. Japanese people started becoming introspectively attracted to Japan's cultural uniqueness and its relationship to other countries, a phenomenon that came to be dubbed *nihonjinron,* or literally, "the theory of the Japanese people." Hammond (1997), in writing on this subject, discussed how some scholars see in *nihonjinron:*

> a Japanese reversal of old power relations between the West and the once subservient Orient ... the last laugh of a nation which once bore the brunt of Western contempt for Orientals, but which now takes its place as one of the world's leading powers. Nihonjinron is merely the mechanism whereby the Japanese take the Western, Orientalist outlook and reverse it upon the West itself. (p. 49)

actions or decisions that the United States was insisting on, the news items did not frame Japan's action or decision as stemming from U.S. pressures, but rather, as coming from Japan's desire to cooperate with the international community. Several references to Japan wanting to cooperate with the United Nations, in the military realm, or with the World Trade Organization, in the economic sphere, were found in these news items (e.g., "Beigun," 1995; "Kome," 1995; "Nichibei Kankei," 1995; "Nichibei Wa," 1995; "Yunyuu," 1995).

Thus, in this time frame of 1975 to 1995, the Japanese news items showed an evolving change with regard to conveyed images. The images changed from reflecting a country that was beginning to sense a degree of confidence, but not to the extent of being able to outwardly challenge the United States, to one of ascending confidence that was able to confront the United States with its own views.[7]

While conveying a change in images of Japan, the Japanese news items relayed consistent and unchanging images of the United States during this same time frame. The images of the United States that were conveyed in the news items were consistently that of a country that was no longer as formidable as it had been in the past, a country that was unable to confront its own weaknesses, and a country that refused to relinquish its hold over Japan.

The United States: Weakened, But Still Demanding

From the mid-1970s, real awakening doubts regarding the strength of the United States were increasingly expressed in many of the Japanese news items. The U.S. political defeats and its weakening economy, in particular, were highlighted in many of the items. Together with such references, the news items either alluded to or directly stated the notion that the United States was not taking up its

---

[7]In his examination of popular comic books and movies in Japan, Sato (1992) observed that beginning in the late 1970s and increasing in numbers throughout the 1980s and into the 1990s, many of these media forms conveyed a sense of Japanese confidence and a feeling of being able to go against the United States. He found that several of these books and movies began depicting Americans as villains that the Japanese were able to confront and defeat. For example, in a popular comic book that later became an animated movie, the setting for the story is in the future, yet the theme and storyline are reflective of World War II. The central characters are the futuristic Japanese military officers who are out to save Japan from their Western enemies by fighting from a space battleship named "Yamato," the name of a Japanese battleship that was destroyed during World War II by the Americans. Although the enemies are not directly stated as being Americans, Sato notes that the names used for the enemy officers are similar to the names of American individuals who actually fought during World War II against the Japanese; furthermore, the base of operations for the enemies looks similar to the skyline of New York City. As the ending for the story, the Japanese are the victors; they defeat the enemy. In relating his interview with the creator of the comic book, Sato stated that the purpose of the comic book was to allow the Japanese, in their imaginations, a chance to refight World War II and build a new sense of nationalism.

responsibility to resolve its weakening political and economic position, and instead, was increasingly targeting Japan as its scapegoat (e.g., "Bei Ga," 1983; "Shijou," 1979; "Tenno," 1975).

In one article, the writer described how the "atmosphere in the United States" was becoming increasingly "cool toward Japan," and that many more Americans were becoming critical of Japan due to Japan's rising economic strength. The writer stressed, however, that such criticism and attitude were being viewed in Japan as reflections of the United States's inability to face its own economic downturn and its use of Japan as a "scapegoat" ("Jyuatsu," 1979, p. 2). In another article, the writer quoted Prime Minister Nakasone as stating that the problem did not lie with Japan, but rather with the fact that "'American businessmen, compared to the Japanese, lacked the effort to sell their products'" ("Bei Terebi," 1983, p.1). In the 1990s, even as Japan was beginning to experience its first economic tremors of instability and decline, the United States was still painted as a less formidable nation that needed to deal with its issues at home before blaming Japan for its problems and interfering in Japan's affairs ("Keizai Mawari," 1995).

Along with conveying the image of the United States as being less powerful and as simply using Japan as an excuse for its political and economic problems, throughout this time frame, the Japanese news items also relayed the image of the United States as being highly demanding and obstinate. The United States was depicted as continuously maintaining an imperious attitude toward other nations, in spite of its weakening international position.

The United States as Demanding

Several news items conveyed a sense that the United States was always insisting on taking the leadership position vis-à-vis Japan, and always making demands, not only in the realm of military affairs, but also in economic concerns as well (e.g., "Fumeirou," 1975; "Jizen," 1975; "Jyuurokunichi," 1995; "Nihon Tataki," 1987). In an editorial expressing dissatisfaction with the methods used by the United States to place various demands on Japan, the writer asserted:

> What I would like the United States to self-reflect on is, first, its high-pressure foreign policy tactics. The United States appears to simply think that in order to make Japan concede, it only has to speak high-handedly and degrade Japan, but this only has the reverse effect. If one incurs the emotional opposition of the Japanese people, issues that were on the verge of reaching agreement could even fall apart. ("Nichibei Koushou," 1979, p. 4)

Also alluding to the pressure tactics of the United States, in another editorial regarding President Jimmy Carter's visit to Japan and the assorted demands the president brought, the writer stated in a cynical fashion, "The only things that weren't brought were the black ships" ("Yomiuri," 1979b, p. 1).[8]

Even in the late 1980s and 1990s, the characterization of the United States as demanding did not change. In one article, the United States was described as being unable to shake its thought of always being "number one" and, therefore, as being unable to realistically deal with its shortcomings ("Nichibei Masatsu," 1987, p. 4). In an editorial, the "black ship" analogy was again used. Referring to the several demands that the United States was making toward Japan regarding economic trade, the writer asserted that the United States's "black ships are endless" ("Shinraundo," 1991, p. 11). In yet another editorial, the writer criticized the United States for its threats of imposing punitive tariffs on Japanese autos and computer chips; the writer asserted that the United States should stop its "arbitrary interference" in the affairs of other countries ("Nijyuu Seiki," 1995, p. 3). In a similar vein, another editorial writer complained that the United States still thought of itself as being the "world police," and thus became involved in the affairs of other countries ("Keizai," 1995).

Several of the news items that referred to the United States's demanding attitude toward Japan often attributed the attitude to the inherent reactive nature of the United States (e.g., "Keizai To," 1983; "Nichibei Keizai," 1979; "Nichibei Tsusho," 1983; "Riken," 1983). For example, one journalist wrote that the United States had a tendency to be friendly to Japan when Japan listened to its demands, but that it reacted harshly when Japan opposed. Within the context of agricultural and automobile imports from Japan, the journalist went on to write that the United States was overreacting to imports from Japan; the journalist stated that Americans had the "emotional opinion that 'Japan is getting fat by feeding off of the United States'" and that many Americans were viewing the imports from Japan as the "'second Pearl Harbor attack'" ("Nichibei Masatsu," 1983, p. 7). In another editorial, the writer stated that the United States was carrying out trade actions toward Japan based on its negative emotional fervor ("Nichibei Koushoudan," 1979).

This notion of the United States as being reactive appeared to intensify in the 1980s and 1990s. For example, one editorial writer declared that although it

---

[8]Note that the "black ships" being referred to in this editorial are being used metaphorically. The black ships refer to the four squadrons of black ships that accompanied Commodore Matthew C. Perry in his mission, on behalf of the U.S. government, to force Japan to establish trade relations with the United States in 1853 (Hall, 1982). Up until that point, Japan had been closed off from the outside world under the seclusion policy of Japan's Tokugawa government's centralized authority. For 250 years, Japan closed its doors to foreign nations. Through threat of force, however, Perry succeeded in his mission of opening up Japan to the outside world in terms of diplomacy and trade, and in 1854, Japan opened its doors to the outside world. The black ships came to symbolize for the Japanese "the new capacity of the Western powers to violate at will the land" of Japan.

may be true that Japan needed to reduce its trade surplus with the United States, the United States needed to become more "judicious" in its decision making regarding Japan ("Reiseisa," 1987, p. 3). One editorial writer stated that the United States was "emotional" in its dealings with Japan, and that it continued to bash Japan because of its emotionality, but that "Japan's generosity" in making concessions to the United States would "someday be repaid" ("FSX," 1987, p. 3). In a similar tone, another editorial writer stated that Japan was tired of the United States's "emotional outbursts" ("Nichibei Chansu," 1987, p. 3). Following the Gulf War, several of the editorials referred to the United States as not behaving "pragmatically" and as getting back at Japan, through trade decisions and actions, because it was "upset" at Japan for not taking up a larger role during the Gulf War conflict (e.g., "Bei Daitouryou," 1991; "Gikai," 1991; "Nichibei Kankei," 1995).

Themes of War

It was during this time when the United States's demands were increasingly conveyed in the Japanese news items as stemming from the United States's reactive character, that noticeable references to war-related metaphors also appeared. The atmosphere enveloping U.S.–Japan relations in this later part of the second time frame was described in many of the news items as being "pre-Pearl Harbor" in nature ("Yomiuri," 1987, p. 1; "Yomiuri," 1991, p. 1; "Yuukou," 1991, p. 13). Several of the articles and editorials also spoke in terms of Japan being thought of by the United States as its "new enemy" or "economic enemy," and of Japan and the United States as engaging in a "trade war" (e.g., "Kyoka," 1991, p. 1; "Nihon Shoujun," 1991, p. 2; "Keizai Mawari," 1995, p. 23; "Nichibei Keizai," 1995, p. 4). Thus, the type of war-related metaphors and analogies was quite similar to what appeared in the U.S. news items.

DISCUSSION

At the outset of this research, the primary theoretical suppositions were that consistencies in images of nations could be found in press content, that those images of nations would reflect national identities, and that the images would tend to be consistent across time in spite of political economic changes. In examining press content from the selected U.S. and Japanese newspapers, the findings did show consistencies in images and that national identities appeared to be embedded in these images. However, even with such consistencies, images also tended to shift along with political economic structural changes between the United States and Japan.

In reviewing the major thematic images of the United States and of Japan, as conveyed by the Japanese news items, images of the United States are consistent throughout this time frame, whereas images of Japan change. During the first half of this time frame, from the mid-1970s into the 1980s, Japan was emerging as an economic power by making strides in its capital investments and industrial growth, but was still very much dependent on the United States for direction and assistance, especially in the military arena. It was during this period, as manifested in the news items, that the image of Japan was that of a nation uncertain, hesitating to break its close, but suffocating, bonds with the United States. As time progresses toward the mid-1980s and into the 1990s, however, the articles and editorials conveyed a Japan that had found the strength and confidence to move away from the United States, more toward the international community. In doing so, it was able to more openly express discontent with and opposition against the United States.[9]

Coterminous with these images of Japan, the image of the United States, conveyed in the Japanese news items, was that of a country that was obstinate and unwilling to give up its stronghold over international leadership and power. The United States was depicted as highly demanding and forceful in its tactics. These images were consistent throughout the time frame and the only image that tended to change was the image of the United States as being a mentor; the mentor became more of an adversary from the mid-1980s onward. What these images have in common with the U.S. images conveyed in the U.S. news items is the notion of the United States holding on to power, although the framing of this notion was presented with a positive spin in the U.S. items.

Despite the progressive weakening of the United States during the time frame, peaking from the mid-1980s and into the 1990s as the nation entered a recession and encountered serious political challenges from other nations, the main image that was sustained in the U.S. news items was that of an inherently robust nation. The U.S. newspaper items relayed, throughout this time frame, images of the United States as experiencing economic and political setbacks, yet managing to maintain its world leadership and authority. Regardless of the objective characteristics of weakness that became associated with the United States, the news items conveyed images of the United States as that of a country that was still very much strong and the envy of the world. The images of Japan, as conveyed by the U.S. news items, were the opposite. In spite of Japan's surge in economic and political strength from the mid-1980s and into the 1990s, the U.S. images of Japan were that of a country that was still very much dependent on the United States and as incapable of becoming a world leader in spite of its newly found wealth.

---

[9]This idea of emerging opposition is also expressed by Miyoshi (1991) in his critical analysis of prominent Japanese literature and films. The researcher found that although certain literary and film artists still tend to slip back into Western "hegemonism," by celebrating Western virtues and ideals, a growing segment of Japanese artists are now engaging in serious criticism against the West. As he wrote, "In today's Japan at least, disagreement is the only way toward the recovery of dialogue and argument, without which no serious and meaningful agreement can possibly be found" (p. 188).

Thus, the overall findings suggest that although national identity appeared to be playing a role in the formations of images, with frequent references to the values, norms, and the dispositional characteristics of the nations, the political economic structural conditions also influenced the form of the images. With the political economic conditions changing, the prominent images tended to fluctuate, mainly in the case of Japan.

To clarify, when placing the main thematic images into typological form, it can be seen that, with regard to the images conveyed in the Japanese news items, a shift in images appears to take place. Images reflecting a new sense of confidence among the Japanese emerge toward the later part of the time frame (see Tables 1 and 2).[10] In the examined U.S. news sources, on the other hand, images of the United States and of Japan tended to remain consistent throughout the period. Although still conveying images of the United States as inherently strong and the only viable world leader, the U.S. news items conveyed images of Japan as inherently weak, dependent, and uncertain, as well as unscrupulous in nature. The only change was a more confrontational adversarial image of Japan that emerged in the late 1980s.

It appears that shifts in political economic structural conditions coincided with changes in images only if the changes were toward a positive direction with regard to the nation's image of itself. In other words, if structural conditions tended to support the move in a nation's image of itself toward one of potency and significance vis-à-vis other nations, that nation's images tended to shift. The findings suggest Japan's growing economic strength and world visibility promoted confidence among the Japanese and an image of a nation capable of holding its own position in the international arena. In terms of the United States, even with its international economic and political decline, the positive images of the United States were maintained, while negative images of Japan intensified. Even when structural conditions suggested a weakening of the United States's power, a form of self-preservation, perhaps, sustained the nation's image of itself as still being a formidable leader. The findings appear to show an interplay of national identities and political economic conditions on the formations of images of nations. The political economic conditions

---

[10]Humphries (1995), in his essay on Western images of Japan and Japan's images of itself, discussed a perceived change among Japanese intellectuals in terms of how they view Japan. He wrote of how, although still "haunted by a creeping sense of cultural inferiority," the Japanese are moving toward a fuller consciousness regarding the uniqueness of Japan, and a greater sense of being able to view the world through their own unique lenses, rather than the lenses of those nations that influenced Japan in the past. Borrowing the words of another author, Humphries wrote,

> by the end of the twentieth century, as Japan begins to play a more major role in world events consistent with her economic status ... it should come as no surprise to find the West [i.e., America]... becoming increasingly irrelevant to whatever new understanding of the structure of meaning is to evolve in Japan in the twenty-first century. (p. 393)

TABLE 1
United States News Items

Thematic Images of Japan

* Inherently weak	* Inherently weak
* Uncertain	* Uncertain
* Dependent	* Dependent
* Duplicitous/unscrupulous	* Duplicitous/unscrupulous
* Supporter	* Adversary

1975_____1980_____1985_____1990_____1995

Thematic Images of the United States

* Inherently strong	* Inherently strong
* Benevolent	* Benevolent
* Leader of the "free world"	* Leader of the "free world"

1975_____1980_____1985_____1990_____1995

TABLE 2
Japan News Items

Thematic Images of Japan

* Uncertain	* Confident
* Still dependent on U.S.	* Increasingly independent/internationally oriented
* Gaining political and economic clout	* Holding political and economic clout

1975_____1980_____1985_____1990_____1995

Thematic Images of the United States

* Politically and economically weakened	* Politically and economically weakened
* Demanding	* Demanding
* Unfair	* Unfair
* Mentor	* Adversary

1975_____1980_____1985_____1990_____1995

appeared to only influence the changes in images if those changes were more beneficial to a nation's sense of identity in general.

When placing these findings within the realm of historical research in international communication that has focused on colonial and postcolonial public discourses, although this study focused on press-disseminated images, the findings appear to support the notion that even with the dismantling of colonial institutions, public discourses of colonialism often remain. In addition, the findings broaden this notion by demonstrating that the form of a nation's identity is key in understanding why such discourses subsist in spite of changes in structural conditions between nations. For nations traditionally in positions of power, such as the United States, the identities associated with the nations would most likely be positive, reflecting strength and leadership. Being in place and nurtured over time, it may be difficult to alter such identities even when power is weakened and structural inequities are corrected. Perhaps public discourses of a colonial or imperial era tend to remain, in spite of changes in structural conditions that call into question such discourses, because they are based on identities that feed a sense of national pride. The discourses are resistant to change if change means that the positive identity of a nation might be challenged and disturbed. Once a positive identity is established, with underlying psychological mechanisms of protectionism at work, the identity is difficult to change. Only through a dramatic process, such as a major revolution or wartime defeat of a nation, might the positive identity undergo a transformation.

CONCLUSION

What this study has hopefully contributed is an understanding that when examining images of nations, it is not sufficient to assume that the political economic structures between nations solely determine the images, but that the national identities of the nations in question must also be recognized and addressed. Many studies that have undertaken the challenge of examining images of nations have had a tendency to assume that structure between nations only matters in determining these images. As the findings from this study have supported, structure is indeed an important factor to consider in the formation of images of nations; however, the identities of nations must also be looked at as important sources of these images. The historical developments of nations, in relation to other nations, and how the identities of these nations have formed, changed, or remained obstinate, and under what conditions, need to be further analyzed and applied toward the understanding of press-disseminated images of nations. This study suggests that a nation's sense of identity is manifested in press writings, through conveyed images, and when examined over a broad span of time within the context of historical events researchers may be able to more fully understand not only the complexities involved in the interplay between structural conditions, national identities, and images of nations, but also the important role these images may play in the communication processes between nations.

The main limitation of this study is that it examines press images from a partial chapter in U.S.–Japan relations. An examination of a longer period of time may provide additional insights into the relationship between structure, identity, and images of nations. It would be interesting to do a study that tracks the

U.S.–Japan press images since the inception of relations between the nations in the late 1800s to the present. If such a study encompassing a longer time frame were undertaken, it might reveal a cyclical pattern of emerging and reemerging images triggered by structural shifts. It may be that structural conditions do not necessarily influence changes in images of nations per se, via national identities, but rather only elicit embedded images that lay dormant within already established and unchanging identities.

ACKNOWLEDGMENT

Data material used in this article was drawn from *Press Images, National Identity, and Foreign Policy: A Case Study of U.S.–Japan Relations From 1955 to 1995*, by Catherine A. Luther. Copyright 2001. Used by permission of Routledge, Inc., part of the Taylor & Francis Group.

REFERENCES

Alter, J. (1994, February 28). Karate or just kabuki? *Newsweek, 123*, 65.
Amerika yo shikkari se yo [Shape up America]. (1987, February 28). *Yomiuri*, p. 3.
Anderson, B. (1991). *Imagined communities*. London: Verso.
Anpou kyouka o hitei [Deny the strengthening of the security treaty]. (1975, May 7). *Yomiuri*, p. 1.
Bei daitouryou hounich de kuryou [Anxieties due to the United States president's visit to Japan]. (1991, March 9). *Yomiuri*, p. 2.
Bei ga chumoku san shinkousaku [United States' attention to industry promoting policies]. (1983, January 12). *Yomiuri*, p. 9.
Beigun tandoku kunren fukumu [Including independent United States military exercises]. (1995, December 9). *Yomiuri*, p. 1.
Bei, hoppo roudo ni kanshin? [The United States interested in the northern islands?]. (1979, April 9). *Yomiuri*, p. 1.
Bei - shouheki houkoku - ni hanronsho [A counter-argument report to the United States' barriers report]. (1995, April 12). *Yomiuri*, p. 7.
Bei suuchi meiji ni koshitsu [The United States insisting on stated numerical target] (1995, June 28). *Yomiuri*, p. 6.
Bei terebi de "Nakasone Bushi" [On American television, "Nakasone's point"]. (1983, January 17). *Yomiuri*, p. 1.
Boeki, boei mo gidai [Defense and trade the subject of discussion]. (1983, November 9). *Yomiuri*, p. 1.
Bookmiller, R., & Bookmiller, K. (1992). Dateline Algeria: U.S. press coverage of the Algerian war of independence 1954–1962. In B. Hawk (Ed.), *Africa's media image* (pp. 62–76). New York: Praeger.
Boyd, G. (1987, April 14). U.S. tariffs against Japan expected. *New York Times*, p. D7.
Buckley, R. (1992). *U.S.–Japan alliance diplomacy 1945–1990*. Cambridge, England: Cambridge University Press.
Buhin uwazumi de tairitsu [To confront with the top of the products]. (1995, April 19). *Yomiuri*, p. 2.
Buki gijitsu, Reagan honichimae ni [Military technology, before Reagan's visit to Japan]. (1983, September 14). *Yomiuri*, p. 2.

Chakuzitsu ni amerika banare [Steadily separating from America]. (1979, February 19). *Yomiuri,* p. 1.
Chang, T. K. (1993). *The press and China policy.* Norwood, NJ: Ablex.
Chip makers assail Japan. (1987, February 10). *New York Times,* p. A21.
Christopher, R. (1987, April 1). Micro-victory in the chip war. *New York Times,* p. A31.
Christopher, R. (1989, February 27). Terms of estrangement. *Newsweek, 113,* 47.
Church, G. (1993, July 19). Traveling salesman. *Time, 142,* 26–27.
Clines, F. (1983, November 15). Reagan returns from Asia trip, looking to a "more secure peace." *New York Times,* p. A4.
Dahlby, T. (1979, June 3). U.S.-Japanese pact on sales is reached. *New York Times,* p. A9.
De Beaugrande, R. (1985). Text linguistics in discourse studies. In T. van Dijk (Ed.), *Handbook of discourse analysis* (Vol. 1, pp. 41–70). London: Academic.
De Lange, W. (1998). *A history of Japanese journalism.* Tokyo: Japan Library.
Deming, A. (1975, October 6). Japan faces up to reality. *Newsweek, 86,* 53.
Deming, A., Kirsher, B., & van Voorst, B. (1975, October 6). Japan faces up to reality. *Newsweek, 86,* 42–44.
Desmond, E. (1994, February 14). In need of a break. *Time, 143,* 46.
The dollar's down. Why not the deficit? (1987, April 28). *New York Times,* p. A30.
Enough U.S.-Japan poison. (1987, June 17). *New York Times,* p. A31.
Fairclough, N. (1992). *Discourse and social change.* Cambridge, England: Polity.
Farnsworth, C. (1987, December 5). U.S. will delay retaliation on Japan construction bans. *New York Times,* p. A37.
Farnsworth, C. (1991, May 3). U.S., Japan reach pact on exports. *New York Times,* p. D1.
Faux, J. (1987, August 31). Here lies free trade. *New York Times,* p. A1.
Ferguson, C. (1987, August 18). Sink or swim with semiconductors. *New York Times,* p. A25.
Fiske, S., & Taylor, S. (1991). *Social cognition.* New York: McGraw-Hill.
FSX o kyouryoku no moderu ni [Making FSX the model of technological cooperation]. (1987, October 4). *Yomiuri,* p. 3.
Fukui, H. (1992). The Japanese state and economic development: A profile of a nationalist-paternalist capitalist state. In R. Appelbaum & J. Henderson (Eds.), *States and development in the Asian pacific rim* (pp. 199–225). Newbury Park, CA: Sage.
Fumeirou da—Yatou hanpatsu [It's unclear—The opposition parties oppose]. (1975, July 23). *Yomiuri,* p. 3.
Gellner, E. (1983). *Nations and nationalism.* Oxford, England: Blackwell.
Gerbner, G. (1991). The image of Russians in American media and the "new epoch." In E. Dennis, G. Gerbner, & Y. Zassoursky (Eds.), *Beyond the cold war* (pp. 31–35). Newbury Park, CA: Sage.
Gikai no fumandaiben [Congress' acting out of dissatisfaction]. (1991, March 23). *Yomiuri,* p. 7.
Gitlin, T. (1980). *The whole world is watching.* Berkeley: University of California Press.
Greenhouse, S. (1995, April 19). Japanese issue threat to quit talks on cars. *New York Times,* p. D1.
Greenwald, J. (1988, July 4). From superrich to superpower. *Time, 132,* 29.
Grove, A. (1987, August 18). Winning the trade war, regain leadership by working together. *New York Times,* p. C3.
Gwetzman, B. (1983, November 13). Diplomatically, Asia is a luxury trip. *New York Times,* p. B2.
Haberman, C. (1983a, November 7). Reagan's trip to Japan: Ties remain strong. *New York Times,* p. A1.
Haberman, C. (1983b, November 9). U.S. to get Japanese and technology. *New York Times,* p. A3.
Haberman, C. (1987, April 28). Eve of U.S. trip: Nakasone packs gifts and woes. *New York Times,* p. A14.
Hall, J. W. (1982). *Japan: From prehistory to modern times.* New York: Dell.
Halloran, R. (1975, September 11). U.S. envoy urges stronger Tokyo ties. *New York Times,* p. A10.
Hammond, P. (1997). *Cultural difference, media memories.* London: Wellington House.
Haruhara, A., & Amenomori I. (1994). Newspapers. In *About Japan* (pp. 13–38). Tokyo: Foreign Press Center.

Hashem, M. (1995). Coverage of Arabs in two leading U.S. newsmagazines: Time and Newsweek. In Y. Kamalipour (Ed.), *The U.S. media and the Middle East* (pp. 151–162). Westport, CT: Greenwood.
Hermann, R. (1985). Analyzing Soviet images of the United States. *Journal of Conflict Resolution, 29*, 665–697.
Hillenbrand, B. (1991, April 8). In search of a triumph. *Time, 137*, 42.
Hillenbrand, B., & Walsh, J. (1991, December 2). Fleeing the past? *Time, 139*, 70.
How about an informal U.S. Japan, inc. (1987, April 28). *New York Times*, p. A31.
Humphries, J. (1995). Images of the floating world: The idea of Japan. *The Antioch Review, 53*, 389–410.
International Press Institute (1972). *The flow of news*. New York: Arno Press.
Japan drifts in several directions at one time. (1975, September 21). *New York Times*, p. D3.
Japanese competition can be healthy. (1983, May 1). *New York Times*, p. C3.
Japanese fearful of conflict in Korea. (1975, May 14). *New York Times*, p. A17.
Jishu kounyuugaku 200 oku doru ni [Independent purchases reach 20 billion dollars]. (1995, June 11). *Yomiuri*, p. 2.
Jizen kyougi kudouka [Don't reduce advanced discussions to pure form]. (1975, July 1). *Yomiuri*, p. 1.
Jyuatsu kakaru: Ohira hobei [Putting the pressure on: Ohira's United States visit]. (1979, April 29). *Yomiuri*, p. 2.
Jyuurokunichi made ni nichibei kyougi [16 more days until Japan-U.S. discussions]. (1995, June 1). *Yomiuri*, p. 2.
Kagou seni mochikoshi [Fiber talks carry over]. (1975, September 12). *Yomiuri*, p. 1.
Keizai chouhousen, sugata arawasu [The figure of an economic intelligence war surfaces]. (1995, October 17). *Yomiuri*, p. 7.
Keizai mawari kanjyou tairitsu mo [Emotions surrounding the economy clash]. (1995, December 7). *Yomiuri*, p. 23.
Keizai to bouei kirihanase [Separate economics and defense]. (1983, January 1). *Yomiuri*, p. 5.
Kijikutsuka e no jika to sekinin [The responsibility and consciousness of being a pivotal currency]. (1995, June 5). *Yomiuri*, p. 3.
Kijuku tsuuka jika to sekinin [Toward a consciousness and responsibility for base currency]. (1995, June 5). *Yomiuri*, p. 3.
Kilborn, P. (1987a, April 16). Hard line by Baker on Japan. *New York Times*, p. D1.
Kilborn, P. (1987b, April 15). U.S.-Japan trade tension mounts. *New York Times*, p. D5.
Kome kaihou jouhou o sokusu [Rice liberalization to promote concessions]. (1995, November 11). *Yomiuri*, p. 1.
Kristoff, N. (1995, June 4). Dutchman strikes chord in a less confident Japan. *New York Times*, p. A12.
Kuruma no teki nousanbutsu de utsu [To strike the auto enemy with agricultural products]. (1995, June 15), *Yomiuri*, p. 2.
Kyoka hoan teishutsu [A strengthened bill for submission]. (1991, November 5). *Yomiuri*, p. 1.
Lacayo, R. (1994, February 24). Clinton to Tokyo: No deal. *Time, 143*, 41.
LaFeber, W. (1997). *The clash: A history of U.S.-Japan relations*. New York: Norton.
Lewis, F. (1991, May 1). The great game of 'gai-atsu'. *New York Times*, p. D25.
Lipset, M. (1990). *Continental divide: The values and institutions of the United States and Canada*. New York: Routledge.
Lohr, S. (1983, May 18). Agency picks growth areas. *New York Times*, p. D1.
Makin, J. (1987, August 30). Our Japan problem and Japan's. *New York Times*, p. C27.
Martin, C. H., & Stronach, B. (1992). *Politics east and west: A comparison of Japanese and British political culture*. New York: Sharpe.
Martz, L. (1989, February 27). Hour of power? *Newsweek, 113*, 15.
Masatsu ga maneku nichibei no tenki [The friction that brings about the turning point in Japan-U.S. relations]. (1987, April 9). *Yomiuri*, p. 3.
Merrill, J. C. (1968). *The elite press*. New York: Pitman.

Miyoshi, M. (1991). *Off center.* London: Harvard University Press.
Mosco, V. (1996). *The political economy of communication.* London: Sage.
Nichibei chansu no ka o fusegu ni wa [In order to reduce the deterioration in Japan-U.S. relations]. (1987, December 15). *Yomiuri,* p. 3.
Nichibei handootai masatsu to kongo no nichibei kankei [Japan-U.S. semiconductor friction and the future of Japan-U.S. relations]. (1987, April 18). *Yomiuri,* p. 3.
Nichibei kankei no akkaboushi ni zenroku o [Giving it all to preventing the deterioration in Japan-U.S. relations]. (1995, December 7). *Yomiuri,* p. 3.
Nichibei keizai dacca no housaku [Plan to break Japan-U.S. economic deadlock]. (1979, February 3). *Yomiuri,* p. 4.
Nichibei keizai kankei o tatenaosu michi [Road to restoring Japan-U.S. relations]. (1995, August 21). *Yomiuri,* p. 3.
Nichibei koushou kecchaku to sougou shugi no gensoku [The principles behind Japan-U.S. negotiation settlement and mutual doctrine]. (1979, June 3). *Yomiuri,* p. 4.
Nichibei koushoudan to shunoukaidan no yukue [Breaking off of U.S.-Japan negotiations and the future of the summit meetings]. (1979, April 27). *Yomiuri,* p. 1.
Nichibei masatsu hibbing teresa [Japan-U.S. friction — unceasing sparks]. (1983, July 7). *Yomiuri,* p. 7.
Nichibei masatsu o kangaeru [Thinking about Japan-U.S. friction]. (1987, April 16). *Yomiuri,* p. 4.
Nichibei tsusho 'ka no jun' wa maemuki ni [Advancement of U.S.-Japan trade]. (1983, September 10). *Yomiuri,* p. 3.
Nichibei wa kinrisaku de kyouchou o isogu [Japan-U.S. rushing cooperation through interest rate policies]. (1995, April 2). *Yomiuri,* p. 3
Nichibei wa sentan sangyou de kyouchou dekiru [U.S.-Japan cooperation can be brought about through cutting edge industries]. (1983, May 24). *Yomiuri,* p. 14.
Nihon shoujun no shintsuushouhoan [New commerce bill targeted at Japan]. (1991, September 11). *Yomiuri,* p. 2.
Nihon tataki ni kajyou hanou suru no [Don't react excessively to Japan bashing]. (1987, December 4). *Yomiuri,* p. 3.
Nijyuu seiki e tsunagu sumitto ni [To the summit that will link to the 21st century]. (1995, June 15). *Yomiuri,* p. 3.
Nokes, R.G. (1990). Libya: A government story. In S. Serfaty (Ed.), *The media and foreign policy.* New York: St. Martin's Press.
Platt, A. (1989, February 27). Shaking the mold. *Newsweek, 113,* 18.
Pollack, A. (1987, April 7). Cuts by Japan now spur fears of chip shortage. *New York Times,* p. D1.
Powell, B. (1989, April 3). To our selves be true. *Newsweek, 113,* 45.
Powell, B. (1991, June 24). A case of ja-panic. *Newsweek, 118,* 33.
Powell, B. (1993, April 26). How tough on Tokyo. *Newsweek, 122,* 40.
Reinhold, R. (1991, September 1). 50 years after Pearl Harbor, reconciliation is still elusive. *New York Times,* p. A1.
Reischauer, E. O. (1995). *The Japanese today.* Cambridge, MA: Harvard University Press.
Reiseisa o kuwake ektite boueki no shitecki [The indication of a lack of rationality in the 'hostile trade']. (1987, February 7). *Yomiuri,* p. 3.
Reston, J. (1979, December 9). Pearl Harbor plus 38. *New York Times,* p. D21.
Riken shinto no aka no nichibei shun kaidansaku [U.S.-Japan summit meeting in the midst of dangerous signs]. (1983, January 16). *Yomiuri,* p. 3.
Rokkan, S., & Urwin, D. (1983). *Economy, territory, identity: Politics of West European peripheries.* London: Sage.
Said, E. (1979). *Orientalism.* New York: Vintage House.
Said, E. (1994). *Culture and imperialism.* New York: Vintage.
Sanger, D. (1995a, June 26). In Geneva, diplomats talk of mufflers, not warheads. *New York Times,* p. A2.

Sanger, D. (1995b, June 30). At the end, U.S. blunted its big stick. *New York Times,* p. D5.
Sanger, D., & Weiner, T. (1995, October 15). Emerging role for the C.I.A.: Economic spy. *New York Times,* p. A1.
Sanjuku ni yugamu sekai keizai to nihon. [Japan and the three handicaps that move the world economies]. (1975, January 7). *Yomiuri,* p. 1.
Sato, K. (1992). *Gojira to yamato to bokura no minshushigi* [Godzilla and yamato, and our own democracy]. Tokyo: Bungeishunshu.
Schudson, M. (1994). Culture and the integration of national societies. In D. Crane (Ed.), *The sociology of culture* (pp. 21–43). Cambridge, MA: Basil Blackwell.
Scott-Stokes, H. (1979, April 29). Japan would like to help, but.... *New York Times,* p. A3.
Sekai antei wasurezu [Not forgetting world stability]. (1983, January 15). *Yomiuri,* p. 1.
Shape up Japan. (1983, January 17). *New York Times,* p. A19.
Shijou kaihou, tsuyoku shingen [Strong suggestion for opening of markets]. (1979, February 10). *Yomiuri,* p. 2.
Shinraundo kobe honkakuka e [Toward a genuine offensive and defensive round]. (1991, May 26). *Yomiuri,* p. 11.
Shitsubo no toki ga kowai [Dreading the time of disappointment]. (1983, January 11). *Yomiuri,* p. 1.
Silk, L. (1987, April 22). On mutual deterrence. *New York Times,* p. D2.
Silverman, D. (1993). *Interpreting qualitative data: Methods for analysing talk, text, and interaction.* London: Sage.
Spurr, D. (1994). *The rhetoric of empire.* Durham, NC: Duke University Press.
Sreberny-Mohammadi, A. (1985). *Foreign news in the media: International reporting in 29 countries.* Paris: United Nations Educational Scientific and Cultural Organization.
Suzuki, K. (1993). *Nichibei kiki to houdou* [The U.S.-Japan crisis and the press]. Tokyo: Iwanamishoten.
Taibei kyouchou o saikyouchou [Intensifying cooperation with the U.S.]. (1975, September 27). *Yomiuri,* p. 2.
Taitou kyouchou no kizuna e [Toward the bonds of cooperation and equality]. (1991, September 8). *Yomiuri,* 1991, p. 1.
Tenno heika gohobei to nihon no yuukou shinzen [Emperor's visit to the United States and Japan's goodwill]. (1975, September 30). *Yomiuri,* p. 5.
Tokyo is caught in the doldrums. (1975, September 14). *New York Times,* p. A5.
A trade crisis highlights mutual resentment and needs. (1987, April 5). *New York Times,* p. D3.
van Dijk, T. (1988). *News analysis: Case studies of international and national news in the press.* Hillsdale, NJ: Lawrence Erlbaum Associates, Inc.
A very important prime minister. (1983, January 17). *New York Times,* p. A1.
Walter, N. (1987). *West Germany's economy.* Washington, DC: American Institute for Contemporary German Studies.
Watson, R. (1991, November 25). Coming to terms with Japan. *Newsweek, 118,* 46.
When spies look out for the almighty buck. (1995, October 22). *New York Times,* p. D4.
Yomiuri Newspaper. (1996). *The Yomiuri Shimbun.* Tokyo: Yomiuri.
Yomiuri sunpyou [Yomiuri review]. (1975a, July 16). *Yomiuri,* p. 1.
Yomiuri sunpyou [Yomiuri review]. (1975b, September 9). *Yomiuri,* p. 1.
Yomiuri sunpyou [Yomiuri review]. (1979a, June 15). *Yomiuri,* p. 1.
Yomiuri sunpyou [Yomiuri review]. (1979b, June 28). *Yomiuri,* p. 1.
Yomiuri sunpyou [Yomiuri review]. (1983, January 20). *Yomiuri,* p. 1.
Yomiuri sunpyou [Yomiuri review]. (1987, April 19). *Yomiuri,* p. 1.
Yomiuri sunpyou [Yomiuri review]. (1991, September 16). *Yomiuri,* p. 1.
Yunyuu kanren yuushi o kakudai [Enlarging the accommodation of imports]. (1995, April 28). *Yomiuri,* p. 7.
Yuukou saistaato no ishizuei ni [Toward the foundations of restarting friendly relations]. (1991, September 7). *Yomiuri,* p. 13.

Shaping Memory of the Past: Discourse in Travel Guidebooks for Vietnam

Scott Laderman
Department of American Studies
University of Minnesota

Asserting that travel guidebooks provide an important generative source of "systems of knowledge and belief" among Western tourists in Vietnam today, the author identifies 3 major discourses in popular guidebooks for Vietnam and concludes that they adhere to a Cold War theme of anti-Communism that assumes American benevolence and criticisms, while allowing for American "mistakes" in the U.S. prosecution of the war, remain within established parameters, contributing to the formation of a certain collective memory of 1 event dominating an era of international communication history.

The 25th anniversary in April 2000 of what the American media consistently referred to as "the fall of Saigon" generated considerable public reflection in the United States about the Vietnamese–American war. According to a *Newsweek* article, the "military commitment that began with a few advisers in the late 1950s to help save the Republic of South Vietnam from the communist North" was "at once a noble cause and a tragic waste that cost 58,000 American lives during more than a decade of fighting and more than 3 million Vietnamese over the course of 35 years of civil war." Although it was a conflict beset by "moral murkiness," it was prosecuted by "well-intentioned policymakers in Washington" (Thomas, Moreau, & Mandel, 2000, pp. 36, 40). An issue of *People Weekly* devoted to the anniversary included an essay by "Ex-POW John McCain on forgiveness," in which he appeared to forgive the Vietnamese for what they did to the United States. The senator celebrated the anniversary while touring Vietnam ("on a trip paid for by NBC") where he reportedly "irritated" his Vietnamese

---

Requests for reprints should be sent to Scott Laderman, Department of American Studies, University of Minnesota, 104 Scott Hall, 72 Pleasant Street, S.E., Minneapolis, MN 55455. E-mail: lade0008@tc.umn.edu

hosts by stating that "the wrong guys won" (Editors, 2000, front cover; Marks, 2000, p. 2; Mydans, 2000, p. A3). *New York Times* editorialists referred to the war as a "senseless conflict [that] might have been avoided," as "[m]ore than 58,000 American servicemen lost their lives in a land of negligible political and economic importance to the welfare of the United States." "[M]ore than anything," they wrote, "the nation must remember this week . . . the needless sacrifice of troops who were betrayed by a president [Lyndon Johnson] who prosecuted a war he did not believe in for a goal that he could not define in public speeches or private conversation." The *Times* editorial suggests the war was "senseless," thus irrational and largely unexplainable, and the project of a single individual—fundamental reanalysis of U.S. foreign policy, then and now, thus appears unnecessary ("A Vietnam Premonition," 2000, p. A30).

Discourses similar to those in such American media coverage pervade representations of the war in travel guidebooks for Vietnam: Among other discourses, the United States was attempting to "help save the Republic of South Vietnam from the communist North"; the war—a "noble cause" yet "tragic waste"—was prosecuted by "well-intentioned policymakers in Washington"; and the American commitment was "senseless." Guidebooks' synopses of the Second Indochina War (what most Americans call the Vietnam War) largely reflect a postwar intellectual consensus that characterizes most mainstream foreign affairs literature. Within this consensus, the U.S. intervention is represented as, in the words of Karnow (1997), "a failed crusade, however noble or illusory its motives," as "America's absolute confidence in its moral exclusivity, its military invincibility, its manifest destiny," abruptly ceased with "Vietnam's conquest by the Communists in April 1975" (pp. 4, 9).[1]

Research for this article about synopses in some of the most popular guidebooks used by Western tourists in Vietnam was prompted by interest in the relationship between historical memory of—and the perpetuation of—empire, particularly the international projection of power by a nation. At the most basic level, the article addresses how historical narratives in major Western guidebooks portray a specific American war—the war in Vietnam. In passing, attention is given to some "dominant fantasies" or "myths" identified by prominent scholars of that conflict, including the myths of "external aggression" (i.e., a Northern invasion of the South) and "military assistance" (i.e., the United States merely assisting the South Vietnamese armed forces (Appy & Bloom, 2001, pp. 55–56; Franklin, 2000, pp. 27–28). At the broadest level, the departure point is scholarly inquiry about the shaping of historical memories and their relationship to later political policies. It is assumed here that a critical consciousness about the past may become disruptive to the persistence of certain forms of policy in the present, and therefore a "doctrinally correct" con-

---

[1]Karnow's text, perhaps the most prominent on Vietnam and the war, was published as the companion volume to a 10-part PBS documentary series, *Vietnam: A Television History*, for which the author served as chief correspondent.

sensus or memory among citizenries is shaped and fostered. In effect, certain memories become necessary for the pursuit of imperial actions.

Collective historical memory here means what Kammen (1997) referred to as "the publicly presented past" in "speeches and sermons, editorials and school textbooks, museum exhibitions, historic sites, and widely noticed historical art, ranging from oil paintings to public sculpture and commemorative monuments" (p. xii). In Western democracies, unlike in authoritarian states in which the government guides the articulation of an official historical narrative, representations in independent media and by nongovernmental historians show—and to a great extent determine—how the past is "remembered." The broadest question posed here, is whether and how historical memory in democratic states is nudged toward what Williams (1980) called a "selective tradition"—or "*the* significant past"— the way in which, "from a whole possible area of past and present, certain meanings and practices are chosen for emphasis, [while] certain other meanings and practices are neglected and excluded" (p. 39).

The work of Lipsitz (1990) on collective memory provides one illustration. Lipsitz has maintained that post–World War II television programmers, to attract a sizable viewing audience, were compelled to acknowledge the persistent memory of prewar class conflict. Although programming's purpose was to make individuals "receptive" to "appeals of advertisers," tension with a popular memory rooted in values of collective struggle and class solidarity challenged program creators to acknowledge and channel that memory towards a capitalist ethos grounded in consumerism. In "evok[ing] the experiences of the past to lend legitimacy to the dominant ideology of the present," Lipsitz contended, programming served as a "vehicle for ideological legitimation of a fundamental revolution in economic, social, and cultural life" (pp. 42, 57). However, Lipsitz noted, the "realism that made urban, ethnic, working-class situation comedies convincing conduits for consumer ideology also compelled them to present alienations and aspirations subversive to the legitimacy of consumer capitalism" (p. 67). Thus, "Even while establishing dominance, those in power must borrow from the ideas, actions, and experience of the past, all of which contain potential for informing a radical critique of the present" (pp. 67–68). The same process is applicable to the U.S. intervention in Vietnam, which most Americans, unlike "opinion leaders," have continued to regard as not just a "mistake" but as "fundamentally wrong and immoral" (Rielly, 1979, p. 79; 1983, p. 98; 1987, pp. 51, 54; 1999, p. 100).

The media generally serve as the major reflectors of a state's doctrinal system and thus function as major contributors to its intellectual culture, but educational institutions and nonmainstream media, including travel guidebooks, also purvey doctrinal "truths." For instance, one study of 28 American high school textbooks found factual inaccuracies or misleading assertions regarding the war in Indochina. They "rarely raise the disloyal and controversial questions necessary to understand the origins and nature of the Vietnam War," the authors wrote:

> Even those textbook authors who are seemingly critical of America's role in the war question it only within a very narrow framework. They rarely raise a fundamental point about the larger purposes of the war, and hence rarely encourage students to attempt a truly critical examination of it. (Griffen & Marciano, 1979, p. 165)

The same could be said of travel guidebooks, for they provide historical synopses that essentially conform to an "already existing story," which is then used to interpret contemporary events, such that, in the words of Abu El-Haj (1998), "key texts and evidence remain in a circular relationship of discovery, explanation, supposition, and proof" (p. 171).

Analyses in Western guidebooks reflect their construction by authors and editors who draw on original scholarship subscribing to disciplinary paradigms. Guidebook texts thus largely reflect, and are constrained by, the parameters of responsible debate within nations' intellectual cultures. Popular historical works about U.S. foreign policy, for example, usually omit imperial intentionality in American foreign affairs, and scholarship generally adheres to notions of the United States as a benevolent—if occasionally blundering—global superpower. Thus is collective memory shaped and perpetuated.

Guidebooks provide an important source for examining collective historical memory, its formation, and its revision. Millions of tourists annually use travel guidebooks, which exist for every region of the globe. The work of Pratt (1992), who studied imperialism and European travel literature using mostly pre-20th-century first-person travel narratives, applies to today's guidebooks. Readers of both travel narratives and guidebooks derive a blueprint for "proper" interpretation of the past and the international system. Pratt wrote:

> How has travel and exploration writing *produced* "the rest of the world" for European readerships at particular points in Europe's expansionist trajectory? How has it produced Europe's differentiated conceptions of itself in relation to something it became possible to call "the rest of the world"? How do such signifying practices encode and legitimate the aspirations of economic expansion and empire? How do they betray them? (p. 5)

Literary scholar Spurr (1993), who also addressed discourses in travel writing, asserted that "despite conventional expectation, [nonfiction] depend[s] on the use of myth, symbol, metaphor, and other rhetorical procedures more often associated with fiction and poetry," and that the "rhetorical modes ... are part of the landscape in which relations of power manifest themselves" (p. 3).

Hundreds of thousands of Western travelers use guidebooks for learning about the places they visit. In countries like Vietnam (or Indonesia or Guatemala or Iran, etc.), tourists may also be turning to guidebooks to learn about the history of their own nations' interactions with these states. What "memory" of U.S. foreign policy will tourists be left with, and to what end will this memory be put? Will it reinforce the belief, as two writers for the *Los Angeles Times* recently asserted, that "America's dominant shadow has long been welcome in much of the world as a shield from tyranny, a beacon of goodwill, an inspiration of unique values" (Marshall & Mann, 2000, p. A1)? Or will it engender critical analysis and political action that affects policy?

Travel guidebooks' synopses convey versions of the past that, through repetition over time, can become a collective memory of an event. Thus is memory of the "significant" past or "selective tradition" shaped, and thus conventional knowledge of events evolves. Considering work by Lipsitz (1990), Spurr (1993), Pratt (1992), and others, tourists' use of guidebooks in Vietnam prompts some important questions: To what extent are the guidebooks incorporating scholarship critical of the United States? Do any, for instance, question what has motivated U.S. interventionism in countries the guidebooks cover? Is there in the synopses any conception of an American empire?

METHOD

Study of travel guidebooks' representations of the war was undertaken to answer this specific question: What discourses about the war appear in travel guidebooks' synopses? In the process of identifying discourses, special attention was given to how the war's history is presented; that is, what reasons are offered, explicitly or implicitly, for the war and how it was executed? What are explanations of U.S. involvement/purposes?

Discourse "points to the fact that social institutions produce specific ways or modes of talking about certain areas of social life, which are related to the place and nature of that institution," according to Kress (1985):

> That is, in relation to certain areas of social life that are of particular significance to a social institution, [discourse] will produce a set of statements about that area that will define, describe, delimit, and circumscribe what it is possible and impossible to say with respect to it, and how it is to be talked about. (p. 28)

Fairclough (1992) wrote that "[d]iscourse is a practice not just of representing the world, but of signifying the world, constituting and constructing the world in meaning," such that—among other constructive effects—"discourse contributes to the construction of systems of knowledge and belief" (p. 64).

Representing a specific media institution in a milieu of contested historiography and memories of the war, Vietnam travel guidebooks help "define, describe, delimit, and circumscribe" (p. 28), in the words of Kress (1985), what can and cannot be said about it. More than just reporting historical facts, guidebooks' representations of the war perform an important function in the construction of historical memory among tourists. It was assumed that identifying discourses in guidebooks may yield insights about memory formation or revision. The most basic assumption underlying the research was that the manner of talking about (explaining and describing) events shapes specific versions of the past and collective historical memory. Thus, fundamentally, it was assumed that travel guidebooks provide one of the most important generative sources of systems of knowledge and belief about a part of American history among tourists in Vietnam today.

To identify discourses, research focused on recurring themes, either explicit or implied, and language that marked a way of talking about subjects. Specific words alone can convey powerful messages—such as *fled* in reference to refugees from North Vietnam (see later); and collections, or groupings, of words convey larger messages—or discourses. Particularly noted were words describing events, giving reasons for the war, explaining U.S. participation and purposes, and the like. Also noted within the discourses were any views critical of the war and the principals involved.

Recent editions of guidebooks by six publishers were examined: Lonely Planet (1993, 1995, 1997, and 1999), Moon (1996, 1997), Rough Guide (1998), Let's Go (1997), Footprint (1997), and Fodor's (*Exploring Vietnam,* 1998; *Vietnam,* 1998). The guidebooks, although giving brief vignettes of most contributors, provide minimal information about authors and editors. As far as could be ascertained, none of these publishers employed Vietnamese writers. The guidebook of Australia-based Lonely Planet was written by an American now residing in Taiwan, an American-Israeli, and an American photojournalist now living in Japan. Both editions of the guidebook by Moon, based in the United States, were written by a British-born Australian now living in Canada. Rough Guide is based in England, and its guidebook for Vietnam was written by a woman described as "[b]orn in Africa" and now living in France, and a man from England who lived briefly in Singapore. The guidebook of publisher Footprint, also based in England, was edited by an Indian-born, Hong-Kong–raised man now living in Southeast Asia, an educator in England described as having "written numerous articles on Vietnam and Southeast Asia," and an artist whose place of birth and current residence are not indicated. United States–based Let's Go provides virtually no substantive information about the two authors of the guidebook's Vietnam section. Fodor's, headquartered in the United States, published two different guidebooks. Its standard "gold" edition was written by an England- and Hong-Kong–raised freelance journalist based in Ho Chi Minh City, several freelance writers for whom no background information is provided, and a New Zealander-American who has lived in Vietnam since 1989 and was formerly executive director of the American Chamber of Commerce in Ho Chi Minh City. The publisher's other guidebook, *Exploring Vietnam,* was written by a travel writer and journalist formerly based in Paris and now living in England.

These are among the most commonly used general guidebooks by English-speaking tourists in the country, and most can be purchased secondhand or as pirated photocopies at bookstalls in major Vietnamese cities. In guidebooks with multiple editions, the pertinent historical synopses changed minimally, if at all, from year to year; later editions, for the most part, had only revised hotel and restaurant listings, transportation timetables, and so on. Because many publishers use the same title—*Vietnam* or some similar designation—the guidebooks are here referred to by publishers' names, rather than by titles, to avoid confusion. Because most tourists tend to purchase guidebooks based on publishers' reputations, publisher "brand" becomes the major selling point and thus signifies degree of potential influence of specific synopses' versions due to circulation levels. In fact, research reported here focused most closely on the Lonely Planet guidebook because of its high circulation, among other reasons.

Lonely Planet's Vietnam and Southeast Asia guidebooks appear overwhelmingly to be the most used by Westerners traveling in that country.[2] Of 94 tourists interviewed throughout Vietnam in June 2000, 74% were using a Lonely Planet guidebook; of the total using a guidebook (10 of the 94 people I spoke with were not) 83% had one published by Lonely Planet.[3] The guidebook of the next closest competitor, Rough Guide, was used by just 7% of those interviewed (and 8% of those using a guidebook). Two percent of the interviewees used the Moon and Let's Go guidebooks, and 4% used Fodor's "gold" edition. No one interviewed was using Fodor's *Exploring Vietnam* or the Footprint guidebook (see Figure 1).

Of the 84 interviewees using a guidebook, 89% (75 persons) said they read guidebooks for historical information about the war. The overwhelming majority (71%, or 60 persons) of those using a guidebook claimed they knew little or nothing about the war before arriving in Vietnam. Nearly 48% of those interviewed were between 20 and 29 years of age, and 23% were between 30 and 39.

Another reason research focused on Lonely Planet is reputation. The publisher capitalizes on its image as a company founded by two backpacker travelers following their 1972 honeymoon "on the 'Hippie Trail' from Europe overland to Asia" (Grossman, 1993, p. 4D). A writer for the London *Daily Telegraph* in 1994 described the publisher's hallmarks as "[g]reat trips, a laid-back, hippy [*sic*] attitude to travel as an adventure, and the sense of being part of an 'alternative' culture" (Gogarty, 1994, p. 37). A writer for the *New York Times Magazine* in 1996 quoted Tony Wheeler—"the multimillionaire cofounder of the Lonely Planet travel empire and trailblazing patron saint of the world's backpackers and adventure travelers"— as saying the company's intended audience is "[i]ndependent-minded travelers"; his wife and cofounder Maureen Wheeler said the publisher markets to "this huge subversive travel market," or the "underground travel market" (Shenon, 1996, p. 34).

---

[2] The Vietnam chapter of the regional Southeast Asia edition is merely an abridged version of the longer and more-detailed Vietnam guidebook.

[3] Again, these could be either Lonely Planet's volume on Vietnam or its guidebook to Southeast Asia. The latter, *Southeast Asia on a Shoestring,* was in its 10th edition at the time of writing.

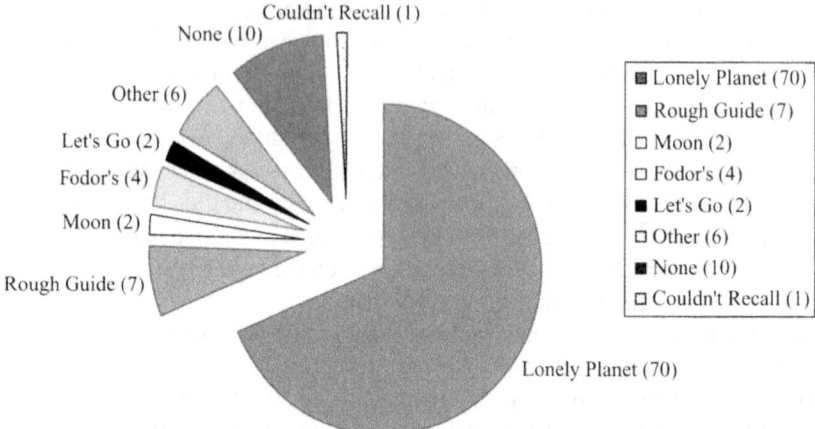

FIGURE 1 Number of persons using guidebooks. Source: Interviews with 94 foreigners traveling or living in Vietnam, June 2000. Note: Total does not equal 94, as some persons were using more than one guidebook.

Every guidebook foreword reinforces the sentiment:

> At Lonely Planet we believe travelers can make a positive contribution to the countries they visit—if they respect their host communities and spend their money wisely. Since 1986 a percentage of the income from each book has been donated to aid projects and human rights campaigns. (Florence & Storey, 1999, pp. 8–9)

More specific about the recipients of the publisher's donations, "The Lonely Planet Story," previously printed on the last page of older volumes, asserted:

> The people at Lonely Planet strongly believe that travelers can make a positive contribution to the countries they visit, both through their appreciation of the countries' culture, wildlife, and natural features, and through the money they spend. In addition, the company makes a direct contribution to the countries and regions it covers. Since 1986 a percentage of the income from each book has been donated to ventures such as famine relief in Africa; aid projects in India; agricultural projects in Central America; Greenpeace's efforts to halt French nuclear testing in the Pacific; and Amnesty International.

A final reason for focusing on Lonely Planet is the publisher's claim for generating responsible tourism practices. Lonely Planet—the "world's largest independent travel guide publisher" within a global tourism industry that generates billions of dollars annually—is explicitly identified as having played a "positive part" in the social and cultural changes spawned by mass tourism (Shaw, 1999, p. 26; Wheeler, 1999, p. 54). But the publisher rejects claims that tourists should avoid egregious violators of human rights such as Burma [Myanmar]—where the democratically elected government-in-exile has called for a tourism boycott—that derive foreign currency from international visitors. "I think bringing tourists in forces governments to lighten up," Maureen Wheeler has stated (Shenon, 1996, p. 34).

The Lonely Planet guidebook message reaches more people than those of the other guidebooks. Other publishers are referred to here when their treatment of the country's history of warfare with the United States shows substantial deviation or when their characterizations of an event or location seem particularly noteworthy.

FINDINGS

The discourses identified in the guidebooks reveal that the U.S. role in Indochina has been viewed largely through a Cold War lens of anti-Communism that assumes American benevolence. Three major discourses were identified around (a) the basis for the U.S. intervention, (b) a "North–South" framework in identifying the "sides," and (c) atrocities and general conduct during the war.

The historical narratives in all guidebooks examined share sufficient characteristics to show a fairly consistent version of the war, but a few differences appear. The first major discourse, identified here as "The Spread of the Reds," ascribes the reason for U.S. intervention to concerns about global Communist expansion. A critical perspective is lacking; for example, only one reference was found to the idea that the war may have been inspired by concerns of empire. That was a misleading comment in a sidebar about why the United States chose not to launch a ground invasion of the North: "[T]here was mounting international criticism that the U.S.A. was simply engaging in imperialism, trying to subjugate Vietnam as its colony" (Florence & Storey, 1999, p. 294).[4]

The second discourse, called here "Establishing 'Sides,'" presents a "North–South War" framework that implies a two-state civil conflict (thus precluding consideration of the war as a U.S. invasion of South Vietnam directed against the

---

[4]Although critics of the war were numerous and intellectually and politically diverse, and someone may have alleged that the United States sought to make Vietnam a U.S. "colony," to my knowledge no such contention appears among what many antiwar activists and scholars consider the most articulate expressions of reasoned opposition. The "imperialist" critique is more complex and has nothing to do with Vietnam's assignment as a "colony"—in the most traditional conceptions of the term. See, for example, the analyses by Young (1991), Kolko (1985), and Chomsky (1982).

southern Vietnamese people). Finally, "Bloodbaths and Aggression," a third major discourse, points up an important difference in the Lonely Planet guidebook's descriptions of the two designated sides in the conflict. Discussion of each discourse in turn includes background and allusion to scholarly accounts for context and clarification in some instances.

Discourse 1: The Spread of the Reds: Why the United States Intervened in Vietnam

Lonely Planet's guidebook content discusses the U.S. intervention in terms of the domino theory—that is, to prevent Vietnam and neighboring Asian states from "falling" like dominoes to international communism. According to the guidebook (Florence & Storey, 1999):

> The theory [was] rapidly gaining acceptance in the west that there was a worldwide Communist movement intent on overthrowing one government after another through various "wars of liberation." Known as the Domino Theory, it gained considerable support after the start of the Korean War in 1950, and the Americans saw France's colonial war in Indochina as an important part of the worldwide struggle to stop Communist expansion. (p. 26)

The domino theory is not subjected to critical scrutiny in the guidebook, and no alternative theory is suggested, although several prominent historical texts offer differing explanations. Also unexplained is how French colonialism—which is recognized as such—shed its imperial qualities during the American subsidization and inheritance of the French Indochinese project.

Vietnam as a "domino" in this discourse of the spread of communism is reinforced in several ways. For example, the publisher noted that by 1973, when most U.S. military personnel were pulled from the territory, "the foreign powers continued to bankroll the war," and "America supplied the South Vietnamese military with weapons, ammunition and fuel while the USSR and China did the same for the North" (Florence & Storey, 1999, p. 31). Elsewhere, it is noted that "[a]s far as anyone knows, the Soviet Union and China—who supplied all the weapons to North Vietnam and the VC—did not suffer a single casualty" (Florence & Storey, 1999, p. 30). Both statements—the latter one false—suggest an equivalence of roles between the United States and the governments of the world's two major communist-led states. (The Lonely Planet authors overstate the extent of Soviet and Chinese support. "The DRV's [Democratic Republic of Vietnam, or 'North Vietnam'] material commitment to the southern resistance, which the southern leaders welcomed, was far from total. The Party always stressed self-sufficiency in arms, to be achieved mainly by capturing them. In 1961 no Soviet or Chinese arms were taken from the NLF [National Liberation Front, or 'Viet Cong'], and in 1963 the

United States claimed that 8 percent of the NLF arms were Sino-Soviet, the remainder being American, French, or homemade" [Kolko, 1985, p. 140].)

This discourse pervades the competitors' guidebooks examined. The Moon guidebook, for instance, provides a fuller development of the paradigmatic framework found in Lonely Planet:

> Vietnam became the linchpin in the U.S. attempt to stop communist expansion in Southeast Asia. The late 1940s and early 1950s were the time of the Cold War, when the Soviet Union and the United States squared off across the globe. After the communist takeover of China in 1949 and the start of the Korean War in 1950, anticommunist hysteria reached fever pitch in the United States. Ho Chi Minh was identified as part of the communist conspiracy, cleverly manipulated by Moscow. In 1954, President Dwight Eisenhower expounded the "domino theory": if Vietnam succumbed to communism, other Asian nations would fall like dominoes, until even Australia was threatened. American strategy was to build up the South Vietnamese army so it could prevent invasion from the north across the 17th parallel. To this end, from 1956 on, American advisers were sent to the south to train the Army of the Republic of Vietnam (ARVN). (Buckley, 1997, p. 63)

The discourse in Let's Go reinforces the same version of Cold War U.S. interventionism: "With the withdrawal of the French came the arrival of the Americans, who assumed responsibility for the survival of democracy by providing financial aid and military advice to South Vietnam" (Yang, 1997, p. 730). A variation here, however, says the United States is seeking "the survival of democracy," following the popular American consensus of the Cold War as a global battle between "freedom" (the United States and its allies) and "totalitarianism" (China and its allies and the Soviet Union and its allies). This implies the Vietnamese nationalists' inclusion in the latter grouping but overlooks the nationalists' advocacy of nonalignment in the Cold War balance of power; and it almost entirely omits the National Liberation Front's 10-point program advocating "a neutral foreign policy" for the South (Young, 1991, p. 70). (The guidebook designation "Communists" for the NLF and North Vietnamese forces is not used here because the NLF represented a broad alliance that included many non-Communists. "Nationalists" here does not mean there were no nationalists in, or supporters of, the Saigon government; however, the scale and variety differed greatly from the ranks of its opponents.)

Young (1991) noted that the program "remained remarkably constant" from its 1960 inception to 1975 and that it called for "the establishment of normal relations between the 'two zones'—North and South— 'pending the peaceful reunification of the fatherland'" (p. 70). The Lonely Planet guidebook makes a brief reference to the Southern nationalists' call for neutralization in its observation that "Hanoi announced the formation of the National Liberation Front, whose political platform called for a neutralization of Vietnam, the withdrawal of all foreign troops, and gradual reunification of the North and South" (Florence & Storey, 1999, p. 25). However, there is no evaluation of what this meant to the American war effort or its implications for the publisher's North–South War framework, nor is there mention in the historical synopsis of the repeated NLF proposals for a negotiated settlement to the conflict.

The discourse in Fodor's *Exploring Vietnam* conforms to the traditional paradigm: The United States came to the assistance of the French because Washington was "[o]bsessed by the spread of the Reds after the success of communist North Korea in 1948 and Mao's Chinese triumph in 1949" (Dunlop, 1998, p. 43).

Of the various guidebooks studied, that published by Rough Guide, although conveying the same discourse, probably comes closest to offering an alternative explanation for the U.S. intervention:

> Behind [American] policies lay the fear of the chain reaction that could follow in Southeast Asia were South Vietnam to be overrun by communism—the so-called Domino Effect—and, more cynically, what this would mean for U.S. access to raw materials, trade routes, and markets.

Notwithstanding this slight deviation, the Rough Guide, like its competitors, neglects the "demonstration effect" that successful revolutionary development could offer to other colonial territories or "underdeveloped" states; its synopsis concludes that the conflict widened "into an ideological battle between the superpowers, fought out on Vietnamese soil" (Dodd & Lewis, 1998, pp. 405–406).

Discussion of Discourse 1. Several Western scholars have suggested that a domino theory was operative in Vietnam, but with far different implications than as framed in the guidebooks. A discourse resting on a domino theory of global communist expansionism omits any challenge to the mainstream Western consensus regarding American foreign policy. Thus, the guidebook publishers neglect the opportunity to critically interrogate U.S. militarism in a broader sense. Young (1991), implicitly rejecting the discourse to which the guidebook publishers subscribe, said that, in "the largest sense, the United States was in Vietnam as a crucial part of the enterprise of reorganizing the post-World War II world according to the principles of liberal capitalism" (p. ix). Chomsky (1982), borrowing from the documented American record, also offered an alternative explanation. He outlined what he viewed as the "basic theme" behind the U.S. intervention:

> Southeast Asia must be integrated within the U.S.-dominated global system to ensure that the needs of the American economy are satisfied, and also the specific needs of Japan, which might be tempted again to set its independent course or to flood Western markets unless granted access to Southeast Asian markets and resources, within the overarching framework of the Pax Americana—the Grand Area. These principles were firmly set by the 1950s and guided the course of the American intervention, then outright aggression, when the Vietnamese, like the Iranians [under Mossadegh], went "berserk with fanatical nationalism" [*New York Times* editorial of

August 6, 1954], failing to comprehend the sophisticated Grand Area concepts and the benefits of "partnership" with the industrialized West. (p. 100)

Kolko (1985) concurred, observing that the "Vietnam War was for the United States the culmination of its frustrating postwar effort to merge its arms and politics to halt and reverse the emergence of states and social systems opposed to the international order Washington sought to establish" (p. 547). Far different from the discourse in the guidebooks studied, these scholars substitute for the global Communist conspiracy (by the Soviets and Chinese) America's need to undermine incipient revolutionary systems (dominoes) that offer development models outside the U.S.-managed capitalist order. In sum, Young, Chomsky, and Kolko situated the American action as *offensive,* an important component of the postwar system of "Grand Area" global management that the United States sought to impose. The discourse in the travel guidebooks, however, suggests that the U.S. intervention was *defensive,* as U.S. policy, according to the synopsis of Lonely Planet, "largely became a knee-jerk reaction against whatever the Communists did" (Florence & Storey, 1999, p. 26).

Discourse 2: Establishing "Sides": The Belligerents in Vietnam

The second major discourse identified in the guidebooks, that of the North–South War belligerents, treats the United States as merely an intervening party in an extant Vietnamese civil war. Although some evidence exists that the Vietnamese dispute was in part a civil war, the totalizing discourse identified in the guidebooks minimizes the leading role assumed by the United States in the conflict. Some historical background is needed for elucidating this discourse, which pervades the guidebooks' treatment of the belligerents.

Central to the American effort in Vietnam was legitimating the establishment of the South as a permanent and separate state. The origin of the North–South divide lay in the 1954 Geneva Conference attended by delegations from France, Great Britain, the United States, the Soviet Union, China, Cambodia, Laos, and Vietnam. The Lonely Planet synopsis accurately says that that international meeting "provided for ... the temporary division of Vietnam into two zones at the Ben Hai River (near the 17th parallel)," but fails to mention that the "two zones" were to be reunified following "nationwide elections" in July 1956 (Florence & Storey, 1999, p. 24). The 1956 elections' purpose was crucial, as they represented, according to political scientist Kahin (1986), the "major *quid pro quo* won by the Viet Minh [i.e., the Vietnamese nationalist coalition that fought against the French colonialists]" in agreeing in 1954 to "regroup[] their military forces to the north of the seventeenth parallel into a territory considerably smaller than the total area they actually controlled." The guarantee of elections transferred "the struggle for the control of Vietnam ... from the military to the political level, a realm in which the Viet Minh leaders knew their superiority over the French and their Vietnamese collaborators was even greater than it was militarily." The Vietnamese nationalists thus "had the assurance that in two years they would have the opportunity of winning control over the whole country through a nationwide election that they were, with good reason, confident of winning" (p. 61).

Whereas the Lonely Planet synopsis states that the 1954 division was to be temporary (without disclosing the 1956 prescription for reunification), several guidebooks contain erroneous claims about the Geneva Accords. This sets the stage for a fundamental misanalysis of why a Vietnamese movement emerged to resist the Americans. The publisher Footprint asserts that "the French and Vietnamese agreed to divide the country along the 17th parallel, so creating two states" (Colet & Eliot, 1997, p. 46). In fact, the accords did not call for the creation of "two states"; they explicitly rejected this, instead calling for two "regrouping zones" with a "military demarcation line [that] is provisional and should not in any way be interpreted as constituting a political or territorial boundary" ("Final Declaration of the Geneva Conference," cited in Gettleman, Franklin, Young, & Franklin, 1995, p. 75). The Let's Go synopsis inaccurately maintains that Vietnam was "divided temporarily along the 17th parallel into two countries," and then correctly asserts that an "all-Vietnamese election scheduled for 1956" was intended "to unify the country" (Yang, 1997, pp. 729–730).

The guidebooks' discourse of a North–South War in Vietnam establishes "sides" in several ways. Stylistically, several headings of the Lonely Planet history section illustrate this discourse: "Franco-Viet Minh War," "South Vietnam," "North Vietnam," "The North-South War," "Enter the Americans" (Florence & Storey, 1999, pp. 24–26). The headings give no indication that the major thrust of the conflict involved the United States (which created and maintained the government in Saigon) and an indigenous southern resistance movement—which was joined only from 1964 onward by regular North Vietnamese troops, although the government in Hanoi had, prior to that time, played an important role in its direction and leadership.

The complex post-Geneva synopsis in the Lonely Planet, as noted, begins with sections covering South and North Vietnam, the two "sides" designated in what Kolko (1985) described as "only very superficially a civil war, [as] behind the fragile veneer of one side stood a foreign nation whose support alone made Diem's very existence and repression possible" (p. 92). The territorial designations (absent critical scrutiny) grant a legitimacy to the South and adhere to American attempts to establish by force—what it could not do politically—a separate, independent, and anti-communist state.

"South Vietnam" is a convenient descriptor; however, in Kolko's (1985) words, "legally Vietnam south of the seventeenth parallel under the Geneva Accords of 1954 was an integral part of one nation transitionally divided prior to reunification," and thus enjoyed "neither a legal nor a historical basis" (p. xiii). The statement in Lonely Planet cited in part earlier—that the Geneva Accords "provided for an exchange of prisoners, the temporary division of Vietnam into two zones at the Ben Hai River (near the 17th parallel), the free passage of people across the 17th parallel for a period of 300 days, and the holding of nationwide elections on 20 July 1956" (Florence & Storey, 1999, p. 24)—is the only substantive reference to the Geneva Accords in the guidebook, a remarkable minimalization given the documents' centrality to the ensuing conflict. The caveat Kolko noted does not appear in the Lonely Planet synopsis, although it says that Ngo Dinh Diem, "convinced that Ho Chi Minh would win an election, refused—with U.S. encouragement—to implement the Geneva Accords," which led to his sponsorship of a referendum on his "continued rule . . . that was by all accounts rigged." No examination of the Saigon government's legal and political legitimacy as an independent state appears—and, in fact, such skepticism seems preempted by the statement that "[a]fter Diem declared himself president of the Republic of Vietnam, the new regime was recognized by France, the U.S.A., Great Britain, Australia, New Zealand, Italy, Japan, Thailand, and South Korea" (Florence & Storey, 1999, pp. 24–25). Moreover, the designation "South Vietnam" suggests inaccurately that the Saigon regime represented the people of that territory. However, most southern peasants, who constituted a majority of the southern population, plus a substantial segment of the urban populace, overwhelmingly opposed the Saigon leadership and its representatives throughout the region.[5]

Implicit support for the South's legitimacy as a sovereign state appears in the contention in Lonely Planet that "[a]fter the signing of the Geneva Accords, the South was ruled by a government led by Ngo Dinh Diem, a fiercely anti-Communist Catholic whose brother had been killed by the Viet Minh in 1945," and whose "power base was significantly strengthened by some 900,000 refugees—many of them Catholics—who fled the Communist North during the 300-day free-passage period" (Florence & Storey, 1999, p. 24). The term *fled* is revealing, as is the omission that "over 130,000 Revolutionary regroupees" went north, "fully anticipating to return home within two years, when the reunification elections were held" (Kolko, 1985, p. 98). Several guidebooks report the move to the North. (See Colet & Eliot, 1997, p. 46 ["nearly 90,000 Viet Minh troops along with 43,000 civilians, went N(orth)"]; Buckley, 1997, p. 63 ["about 80,000 people journeyed north"]; and Dodd & Lewis, 1998, p. 405 ["(a)pproaching 100,000 anti-French guerrillas and sympathizers moved in the opposite direction to regroup"].) Young (1991) called the exodus by hundreds of thousands of Catholics to the South of "particular propaganda value to Diem," as the refugees "were said to have 'voted with their feet' for freedom." This sentiment is consistent with use of the word *fled*, which appears to confirm western presuppositions regarding communist terror (p. 45).

---

[5] This fact is critical; at its core, the U.S. intervention symbolized the Americans' failure to undermine the Vietnamese nationalist movement and offer a viable alternative—thus the creation in 1960 of the NLF from the remnants of the Viet Minh.

Discussion of Discourse 2. Omitted from the Lonely Planet guidebook is the role of "black propaganda" by American intelligence in the mass movement of northern Catholics to the South. Under the auspices of the Saigon Military Mission (SMM), led by Central Intelligence Agency (CIA) operative Colonel Edward G. Lansdale, United States–sponsored political-psychological warfare emerged as a substantial component of American policy in 1954, irrespective of its contravention of the Geneva Accords. Among other tactics, the SMM employed economic sabotage and the widespread dissemination of rumors in an effort to destabilize the North.

Of the guidebooks studied, only one mentions the American propaganda campaign. The Rough Guide states:

> Almost a million (mostly Catholic) refugees headed south, their flight aided by the US Navy, and to some extent engineered by the CIA, whose distribution of scaremongering, anti-communist leaflets was designed to create a base of support for the puppet government it was concocting in Saigon. Approaching 100,000 anti-French guerrillas and sympathizers moved in the opposite direction to regroup, though as a precautionary measure, between 5000 and 10,000 Viet Minh cadres remained in the south, awaiting orders from Hanoi. (Dodd & Lewis, 1998, p. 405)

Why hundreds of thousands of Vietnamese would "flee" to the South receives no consideration in the Lonely Planet guidebook. It seems a truism within the American doctrinal system that people naturally seek to escape communist-led societies, so Western tourists, immersed in a Cold War ideological framework of communist savagery and American democracy, would presumably need no explanation. Thus the particular attributes of the Vietnamese revolutionary movement, which enjoyed substantial popular support throughout the nation, went unmentioned.

Lonely Planet's totalizing civil war discourse ultimately leads to internal narrative confusion. For instance, the section on the North–South War begins chronologically with "the mid-1950s" but later notes that, "for the South, it was no longer just a battle with the VC ['Viet Cong,' or NLF]. In 1964, Hanoi began infiltrating regular North Vietnamese Army (NVA) units into the South" (Florence & Storey, 1999, p. 26). What made the conflict a North–South War from "the mid-1950s" to 1964 if the North was not directly engaged in a combat role during that time? Portraying the war as a two-state civil conflict—as opposed to a U.S. invasion of the South—supports Chomsky's (1997) assertion that "we cannot recognize the elementary truth that we attacked South Vietnam—certainly in 1961—and that South Vietnam was the main target of our attack right to the end of the war" (p. 184).

Discourse 3: Bloodbaths and Aggression

The third discourse emerges from the differing treatment of the two designated sides. This difference appears, for instance, in Lonely Planet's treatment of atrocities: The terror of the nationalists is highlighted and graphically conveyed, whereas that of the United States and its proxy seems remarkably sterile. The effect is an ex post facto legitimation of the U.S. intervention. Bloodbaths are portrayed as inherent to communist governance, thus lending moral credibility to what is frequently identified in the United States as the Americans' "defense" of the South. The synopses of the guidebooks, in fact, appear to be not very different from Hallin's (1986) finding about American television coverage of the war, in which the North Vietnamese and NLF were represented by broadcasters in "an almost perfectly one-dimensional image" as "cruel, ruthless, and fanatical" (p. 148).

The "Communists" are blamed in the Lonely Planet guidebook for two major episodes, although subtle criticisms appear throughout the text. The first episode encompasses the brutal land reform atrocities of the mid-1950s—which should be denounced but must be properly understood. The second episode is the so-called Hue Massacre of 1968.

In the discourse, the land reform is framed as an example of communist duplicity, an immediate and bald effort to "eliminate elements of the population that threatened [the new government's] power." The Lonely Planet section entitled "North Vietnam" states:

> The Geneva Accords allowed the leadership of the Democratic Republic of Vietnam to return to Hanoi and to assert control of all territory north of the 17th parallel. The new government immediately set out to eliminate elements of the population that threatened its power. A radical land-reform program was implemented, providing about half a hectare of land to some 1.5 million peasants. Tens of thousands of "landlords," some with only tiny holdings—and many of whom had been denounced to "security committees" by envious neighbors—were arrested. Hasty "trials" resulted in 10,000 to 15,000 executions and the imprisonment of 50,000 to 100,000 people. In 1956, the Party, faced with serious rural unrest caused by the program, recognized that the People's Agricultural Reform Tribunals had gotten out of hand and began a "Campaign for the Rectification of Errors." (Florence & Storey, 1999, p. 25)

No indication was found in the Lonely Planet guidebook that atrocities accompanying the land reform departed from the planners' original goals. Among complex explanations by several scholars, Kolko (1985) wrote, "Until 1956, the land reform organizational structure was functioning not only independently of the Party but often against it, basing its power on the poor peasantry" (p. 66). Young (1991) similarly elucidated how the program spiraled out of control when handled by local officials, as "[a]ncient village grievances, religious differences, petty spite, and a growing paranoia frequently left villages not transformed, but deeply embittered." In what she referred to as "an exceptionally stringent self-criticism," by mid-1956 "Party leaders reexamined the entire course of the reform and set out to correct the abuses." Of particular relevance, Young said the land reform (which increased the holdings in land, tools, and farm animals of 60 percent of the population) and the public rectification of its campaign excesses deepened popular support for the government. As even defectors to South Vietnam tried to instruct the unbelieving Americans who questioned them, "the North has the support of the people." (pp. 50–51)

The executions were embraced years later by U.S. and Saigonese propagandists as evidence of Communist terror and justification for the American intervention in the South. Historian Moise (1983) observed:

> The land reform lasted roughly from December 1953 to July 1956. Throughout that period, the Saigon government was pouring out propaganda about how terrible the Communists were. Yet that propaganda contained very little about the land reform and related matters. In October 1956, Saigon learned from international press agency dispatches that the DRV was admitting that serious land reform excesses had occurred. Only after this did Saigon's anti-communist tracts become filled with supposed eyewitness accounts of mass slaughter in the land reform. (p. 218)

Richard Nixon claimed that 500,000 people had been executed and an additional 500,000 placed in "slave labor camps." The "standard estimate" was that of Bernard Fall, who estimated approximately 50,000 dead. According to Moise (1983), "the total number . . . was probably on the rough order of 5000 and almost certainly between 3000 and 15,000" (p. 222). Given the recognized authority of Moise's study, it is uncertain why Lonely Planet cites Buttinger's (1967) higher estimate of 10,000 to 15,000, which posits a minimum that is 100% greater than the probable figure estimated by Moise (1983, p. 914).[6]

The second major episode, the so-called Hue Massacre of 1968, is described in the historical synopsis of Lonely Planet's section on the ancient imperial capital. Hue was "the only city in South Vietnam to be held by the Communists for more than a few days":

> Immediately upon taking Hue, Communist political cadres implemented detailed plans to liquidate Hue's "uncooperative" elements. Thousands of people were rounded up in extensive house-to-house searches conducted according to lists of names meticulously prepared months before. During the 3 1/2 weeks Hue remained under Communist control, approximately 3000 civilians—including merchants, Buddhist monks, Catholic priests, intellectuals and a number of foreigners, as well as people with ties to the South Vietnamese government—were summarily shot, clubbed to death or buried alive. The victims were buried in shallow mass graves, which were discovered around the city over the next few years. (Florence & Storey, 1999, p. 314)

---

[6]The land reform campaign also appears in the guidebooks by Moon (Buckley, 1997, p. 63), Rough Guide (Dodd & Lewis, 1998, p. 406), Footprint (Colet & Eliot, 1997, p. 96), and the two by Fodor's (Dunlop, 1998, p. 44; Lesser, 1998, p. 243).

The episode, mentioned in every Vietnam guidebook studied except that published by Let's Go, is described in the Footprint guidebook as lending "support to the notion that should the [North] ever achieve victory over the [South] it would result in mass killings" (Colet & Eliot, 1997, p. 175). But the Hue Massacre as reported—"the official story of an indiscriminate slaughter of those who were considered to be unsympathetic to the NLF"—according to the political scientist Gareth Porter (1974), "is a complete fabrication" (p. 11). Porter's study, subsequently entered into the U.S. *Congressional Record,* concluded that the description transmitted years later by Lonely Planet and the other guidebook publishers "bore little resemblance to the truth, but was, on the contrary, the result of a political warfare campaign by the Saigon government, embellished by the U.S. government, and accepted uncritically by the U.S. press" (p. 2).[7] Porter found that a number of executions did take place, but on a scale and in a fashion far different than reported in the guidebooks.

In contrast to the detailed explication of Communist atrocities, Lonely Planet gives little indication, with the exception of the My Lai massacre, that the United States and its client conducted a widespread campaign of terror in the South. Although the publisher enumerates North Vietnamese/NLF atrocities (10,000–15,000 executions and 50,000–100,000 persons imprisoned during the land reform; 3,000 executed during the Hue Massacre), it gives no comparable figures for the Saigon administration nor does it hint that such atrocities were a regular and ongoing feature of American warfare (as the importance of "body counts" to U.S. planners suggests). According to political scientist William Turley (1986), the "number of politically motivated executions in the South during the 1950s probably exceeded the number in the North" (p. 18). Turley cited Kendrick's estimate of 75,000 (p. 32); alone among the guidebooks for Vietnam, the Rough Guide reports "over 50,000" killed (Dodd & Lewis, 1998, p. 405). The writers of the Footprint guidebook implicitly deny that any executions occurred in the South: "Diem's campaign was successful in undermining the strength of the Communist Party in the [South]. While there were perhaps 50,000–60,000 Party members in 1954, this figure had declined through widespread arrests and intimidation to only 5000 by 1959" (Colet & Eliot, 1997, p. 47). Also important in considering atrocities by the Southern regime is that the bulk of the deaths occurred, a former adviser to Ngo Dinh Diem wrote, "more than two years before the Communists began to commit acts of terror against local government officials [in South Vietnam]" (Joseph Buttinger, cited in Kahin, 1986, p. 97).

Discussion of Discourse 3. Through one guidebook's description of a popular attraction in Ho Chi Minh City, one can discern the discomfort in confronting the existence of U.S.-sponsored atrocities. A writer for Fodor's "gold"

---

[7] The study appears in the *Congressional Record* of February 19, 1975.

guidebook cautioned tourists about an institution previously called the "Museum of American War Crimes," later renamed the "War Crimes Museum," and now known as the "War Remnants Museum." (The evolution in name suggests Vietnam's effacement of its national historical narrative for one more palatable to American tourists.) The Fodor's writer said that "[y]ou'll probably come away with mixed feelings about the one-sided propaganda—ashamed of the U.S. actions, angry about the Vietnamese inaccuracies in depicting them, or both." Observing that, even with the name change the museum's "coverage continues to be skewed," the Fodor's writer stated that:

> Conspicuous in its absence . . . is any mention of the division of the country into South Vietnam and North Vietnam. . . . (The Communist government tends to overlook this division; instead it claims a puppet government backed by American imperialists illegally ruled in the South against the will of the people.). (Lesser, 1998, p. 181)

Although war memorials and museums in Vietnam employ a lexicon ("imperialists," "puppets," etc.) making it easy for visitors to dismiss what the sites were intended to convey, the jargon cloaks an alternative narrative.

The Fodor's statement about the American atrocities covered at the museum epitomizes the discourse: "Also missing is information about some of the horrors perpetrated by the National Liberation Front, particularly the 14,000 [?] people massacred in Hue during the 1968 Tet Offensive" (Lesser, 1998, pp. 181). The presumed need to balance U.S. atrocities with those of the Vietnamese nationalists is consistent with the discourse identified in the guidebooks studied. The other Fodor's guidebook, *Exploring Vietnam,* illustrates this: "Diem's police, headed by his neofascist brother Ngo Dinh Nhu, embarked on a ruthless campaign using torture and execution to uproot communist sympathizers and recalcitrant Viet Minh" (Dunlop, 1998, p. 44). Yet although there is no indication how extensive the campaign was, a misleading statement about the nationalists effectively balances the charge against the Saigon regime:

> Things were no better in the North. Catholics fled south and the rest of the population was subjected to brutal land reforms in order to enforce collectivization. Anyone who owned a rice paddy was treated as a bourgeois, his home confiscated and public confessions extracted. Persecutions and 10,000 deaths ended with a governmental volte-face in 1956, when the campaign for the "Rectification of Errors" brought back the popular Uncle Ho [Chi Minh] to initiate more subtle reforms. (Dunlop, 1998, p. 44)

Balance becomes problematic when used to suggest an equivalence ("[t]hings were no better in the North") between the two entities. (The atrocities by the nationalists, which were horrible, nevertheless paled in comparison to those by the Saigon government and its American benefactor.)

In addition to treatment of wartime atrocities, discourse in Lonely Planet distinguishes the two designated sides in subtle ways. For instance, the publisher notes that in January 1975 the North Vietnamese "launched a massive conventional ground attack across the 17th parallel," calling the action "a blatant violation of the Paris agreements" (Florence & Storey, 1999, p. 31). The charge is instructive but requires contextualization. The guidebook introduces the 1973 Paris Agreement by stating that:

> [t]he "Christmas Bombing" of Haiphong and Hanoi at the end of 1972 was meant to wrest concessions from North Vietnam at the negotiating table. Finally, Kissinger and Le Duc Tho [the North Vietnamese representative in Paris] reached agreement. The Paris Agreement [was] signed by the U.S.A., North Vietnam, South Vietnam, and the VC on 27 January 1973. (Florence & Storey, 1999, p. 29)

The statement implies that the "Christmas Bombing" by the United States led to North Vietnamese concessions and the completion of a negotiated settlement. In fact, the B-52 bombing of these urban targets was a domestic political disaster for Richard Nixon; and it has been persuasively argued that the U.S. government was forced to accept an agreement virtually identical to the nine-point proposal presented to Kissinger by Tho in October 1972—itself similar to numerous agreements proposed by the nationalists over the years—and built on the basic structure of the 1954 Geneva Accords. An aide to Kissinger concluded: "We bombed the North Vietnamese into accepting our concessions" (John Negroponte, cited in Young, 1991, p. 279).

The charge regarding the North's "blatant violation" of the Paris Agreement appears in the guidebook without comment on the consistent Saigonese refusal to abide by its provisions or the U.S. role in abetting this series of violations. The Lonely Planet synopsis insinuates that the North launched an invasion of the South in an effort to conquer the territory in "blatant" contravention of the 1973 settlement, but it omits the Saigon regime's repeated "blatant violation[s]" that preceded the January 1975 offensive. Among these, historian Ngo Vinh Long (1991) pointed to three: the consistent Saigonese denial in allowing "any political role" for the Provisional Revolutionary Government (PRG; i.e., the NLF party that signed the accord); the enunciation by the president of South Vietnam, Nguyen Van Thieu, of his Four No's Policy (no recognition of the enemy, no coalition government, no neutralization of the southern region of Vietnam, and no concession of territory); and the "indiscriminate bombings and shellings as well as ground assaults on PRG-controlled areas" by the Thieu government (pp. 44–50). There were, moreover, numerous violations by the United States, beginning with statements regarding South Vietnam's "sovereignty" immediately following the Paris Agreement's ratification by the various parties. (See Chomsky, 1982, pp. 115–125.) None of these contraventions is mentioned in the

Lonely Planet guidebook. Only the 1975 offensive is deemed a "blatant violation" of the accord, framing, once again, a singular malevolence on the part of the nationalists.

CONCLUSION

Although the discourses found in Vietnam travel guidebooks do not, for the most part, sing paeans to America's "noble crusade" in Southeast Asia, as former U.S. president Ronald Reagan adjudged it, they also provide no scrutiny of the reigning shibboleths of the war. A portrait of U.S. foreign policy largely adhering to the conventional strictures of the "containment" paradigm dominates. Thus, Lonely Planet and its competitors reflect an intellectual environment in which "mistakes" are allowed but criticism is contained within certain parameters—aiding and abetting the shaping of a specific collective memory.

ACKNOWLEDGMENTS

Scott Laderman, a MacArthur Scholar and doctoral candidate in the Department of American Studies at the University of Minnesota, would like to thank Hokulani Aikau, Patricia Albers, Karla Erickson, Brett Gary, Lary May, Carol Miller, Edwin Moise, David Noble, Richard Price, Emily Rosenberg, and three anonymous reviewers for *Mass Communication & Society* for their thoughtful comments on different portions of this article at different stages. Many others, including his wonderful graduate student colleagues at Minnesota, also commented on various portions of the project, for which he is extremely grateful. The author, of course, assumes full responsibility for any errors of fact or analysis contained herein.

REFERENCES

Abu El-Haj, N. (1998, May). Translating truths: Nationalism, the practice of archaeology, and the remaking of past and present in contemporary Jerusalem. *American Ethnologist, 25*, 166–188.

Appy, C., & Bloom, A. (2001). Vietnam War mythology and the rise of public cynicism. In A. Bloom (Ed.), *Long time gone: Sixties America then and now* (pp. 47–73). Oxford, England: Oxford University Press.

Buckley, M. (1996). *Vietnam, Cambodia, and Laos handbook* (1st ed.). Chico, CA: Moon Publications.

Buckley, M. (1997). *Vietnam, Cambodia, and Laos handbook* (2nd ed.). Chico, CA: Moon Publications.

Buttinger, J. (1967). *Vietnam at war: Vol. 2. Vietnam: A dragon embattled.* New York: Praeger.

Chomsky, N. (1982). *Towards a new cold war: Essays on the current crisis and how we got there.* New York: Pantheon.

Chomsky, N. (1997). The cold war and the University. In N. Chomsky, et al. (Eds.), *The cold war and the university: Toward an intellectual history of the postwar years*. New York: The New Press.
Colet, J., & Eliot, J. (1997). *Vietnam handbook*. Bath, England: Footprint Handbooks.
Dodd, J., & Lewis, M. (1998). *Vietnam: The rough guide* (2nd ed.). London: Rough Guides.
Dunlop, F. (1998). *Fodor's exploring Vietnam*. New York: Fodor's Travel Publications.
Editors. (2000, May 1). *People Weekly*.
Fairclough, N. (1992). *Discourse and social change*. Cambridge, England: Polity.
Florence, M., & Storey, R. (1999). *Vietnam* (5th ed.). Melbourne, Australia: Lonely Planet.
Franklin, H. B. (2000). *Vietnam and other American fantasies*. Amherst: University of Massachusetts Press.
Gettleman, M. E., Franklin, J., Young, M. B., & Franklin, H. B. (Eds.). (1995). *Vietnam and America: A documented history* (2nd ed.). New York: Grove.
Gogarty, P. (1994, October 8). Lonely Planet—the dog-eared survivor. *Daily Telegraph*, p. 37.
Griffen, W. L., & Marciano, J. (1979). *Teaching the Vietnam war*. Montclair, NJ: Allanheld, Osmun.
Grossman, C. L. (1993, April 1). Guidebooks publishers' lonely planet is growing. *USA Today*, p. 4D.
Hallin, D. C. (1986). *The "uncensored war": The media and Vietnam*. Berkeley: University of California Press.
Kahin, G. M. (1986). *Intervention: How America became involved in Vietnam*. New York: Anchor/Doubleday.
Kammen, M. (1997). *In the past lane: Historical perspectives on American culture*. New York: Oxford University Press.
Karnow, S. (1997). *Vietnam: A history* (rev. ed.). New York: Penguin.
Kendrick, A. (1974). *The wound within*. Boston: Little, Brown.
Kolko, G. (1985). *Anatomy of a war: Vietnam, the United States, and the modern historical experience*. New York: Pantheon.
Kress, G. (1985). Ideological structures in discourse. In T. A. Van Dijk (Ed.), *Handbook of discourse analysis: Discourse analysis in society* (Vol. 4, pp. 27–42). London: Academic.
Lesser, N. (Ed.). (1998). *Vietnam*. New York: Fodor's Travel Publications.
Lipsitz, G. (1990). *Time passages: Collective memory and American popular culture*. Minneapolis: University of Minnesota Press.
Long, N. V. (1991). Vietnam. In D. Allen & N. V. Long (Eds.), *Coming to terms: Indochina, the United States, and the war* (pp. 9–64). Boulder, CO: Westview.
Marks, P. (2000, April 30). A bigger draw than Julia Roberts. *New York Times*, sec. 4, p. 2.
Marshall, T., & Mann, J. (2000, March 26). Goodwill toward U.S. is dwindling globally. *Los Angeles Times*, pp. A1, A30–A31.
McCain, J. (2000, May 1). I've made my peace with Vietnam. *People Weekly*, 116–119.
Moise, E. E. (1983). *Land reform in China and North Vietnam: Consolidating the revolution at the village level*. Chapel Hill: University of North Carolina Press.
Mydans, S. (2000, April 29). Old wounds slow U.S.-Vietnam reconciliation. *New York Times*, p. A3.
Porter, D. G. (1974, June 24). The 1968 "Hue massacre." *Indochina Chronicle, 33*, 2–13.
Pratt, M. L. (1992). *Imperial eyes: Travel writing and transculturation*. London: Routledge.
Rielly, J. E. (1979, Spring). The American mood: A foreign policy of self-interest. *Foreign Policy, 34*, 74–86.
Rielly, J. E. (1983, Spring). American opinion: Continuity, not Reaganism. *Foreign Policy, 50*, 86–104.
Rielly, J. E. (1987, Spring). America's state of mind. *Foreign Policy, 66*, 39–56.
Rielly, J. E. (1999, Spring). Americans and the world: A survey at century's end. *Foreign Policy, 114*, 97–114.
Robinson, D., & Storey, R. (1993). *Vietnam: A travel survival kit* (2nd ed.). Melbourne, Australia: Lonely Planet.
Shaw, J. (1999, January–March). Planet circles the globe. *Europe Business Review, 2*(7), 26.
Shenon, P. (1996, June 30). The end of the world on 10 tugriks a day. *New York Times Magazine*, 34–37.

Spurr, D. (1993). *The rhetoric of empire: Colonial discourse in journalism, travel writing, and imperial administration.* Durham, NC: Duke University Press.
Storey, R., & Robinson, D. (1995). *Vietnam: A lonely planet travel survival kit* (3rd ed.). Melbourne, Australia: Lonely Planet.
Storey, R., & Robinson, D. (1997). *Vietnam.* (4th ed.). Melbourne, Australia: Lonely Planet.
Thomas, E., Moreau, R., & Mandel, A. (2000, May 1). The last days of Saigon. *Newsweek,* 34–42.
Turley, W. S. (1986). *The second Indochina war: A short political and military history, 1954–1975.* Boulder, CO: Westview.
A Vietnam premonition. (2000, April 25). *New York Times,* p. A30.
Wheeler, T. (1999, July–August). Philosophy of a guidebook guru. *UNESCO Courier,* 54–55.
Williams, R. (1980). *Problems in materialism and culture: Selected essays.* London: Verso.
Yang, P. C. (Ed.). (1997). *Let's go: The budget guide to Southeast Asia, 1997.* New York: St. Martin's Press.
Young, M. B. (1991). *The Vietnam wars 1945–1990.* New York: HarperPerennial.